TAKING CONTROL
OF YOUR
COLLEGE READING AND LEARNING

Elaine H. Byrd

Elaine C. Carter

Stacy D. Waddoups

Utah Valley State College

HEINLE & HEINLE

THOMSON LEARNING

Australia Canada Mexico Singapore Spain United Kingdom United States

HEINLE & HEINLE

THOMSON LEARNING

Taking Control of Your College Reading and Learning
Elaine H. Byrd, Elaine C. Carter, Stacy D. Waddoups

Publisher: Earl McPeek
Acquisitions Editor: Stephen Dalphin
Market Strategist: John Meyers
Project Manager: Andrea Archer
Cover design by Jodi V. Waddoups
Cover photography by Annette Coolidge

Printed in Canada

5 6 7 8 9 10 06 05 04

For more information contact Heinle & Heinle, 25 Thomson Place, Boston, MA 02210 USA, or you can visit our Internet site at http://www.heinle.com

For permission to use material from this text or product contact us:
Tel: 1-800-730-2214
Fax: 1-800-730-2215
Web: www.thomsonrights.com

ISBN: 0-15-506375-8

Library of Congress Catalog Card Number:
    00-105030

Harcourt College Publishers

Where Learning Comes to Life

TECHNOLOGY

Technology is changing the learning experience, by increasing the power of your textbook and other learning materials; by allowing you to access more information, more quickly; and by bringing a wider array of choices in your course and content information sources.

Harcourt College Publishers has developed the most comprehensive Web sites, e-books, and electronic learning materials on the market to help you use technology to achieve your goals.

PARTNERS IN LEARNING

Harcourt partners with other companies to make technology work for you and to supply the learning resources you want and need. More importantly, Harcourt and its partners provide avenues to help you reduce your research time of numerous information sources.

Harcourt College Publishers and its partners offer increased opportunities to enhance your learning resources and address your learning style. With quick access to chapter-specific Web sites and e-books . . . from interactive study materials to quizzing, testing, and career advice . . . Harcourt and its partners bring learning to life.

Harcourt's partnership with Digital:Convergence™ brings :CRQ™ technology and the :CueCat™ reader to you and allows Harcourt to provide you with a complete and dynamic list of resources designed to help you achieve your learning goals. You can download the free :CRQ software from www.crq.com. Visit any of the 7,100 RadioShack stores nationwide to obtain a free :CueCat reader. Just swipe the cue with the :CueCat reader to view a list of Harcourt's partners and Harcourt's print and electronic learning solutions.

http://www.harcourtcollege.com/partners

CONTENTS

Preface to the Instructor   ix
Preface to the Student   xv
BICUM Bookmark   xvii
Acknowledgments   xix

1 Taking Control of Your Reading   1

High School Versus College Reading   1
Study-Reading   2
Inactive Reading   3
Developing Metacognition   4
Metacognitive Training   5
Self-, Task-, and Strategy-Awareness   8
Self-Awareness   9
Task-Awareness   11
Strategy-Awareness   12
Believing in Yourself: Self-Efficacy   12
A Study-Reading Plan   16
The Four Stages of BICUM   16
Benefits of Using BICUM   17
Personalize BICUM   19
Summary   21
Review Questions   22
Metacognitive Insights   23

2 Getting Ready to Read   25

SELF Inventory   26
S Stands for **Study Area**   27
E Stands for **Emotions**   30
L Stands for **Level of Difficulty**   31
F Stands for **Feeling Physically**   36
Everyday Physical Care   37
SELF Inventory Results   39
Preview Your Reading   40
Notice the Title   40

Contents

Read the Introduction and Summary   41

Check the Headings and Subheadings   42

Check the Bold and Italicized Print   43

Utilize the Charts, Maps, Graphs, and Diagrams   43

Make Predictions   45

Create an Interest   46

Select or Create Questions   48

Set Study Length   48

Place Control □'s   50

Is Study-Reading for You?   55

Summary   57

Review Questions   58

Metacognitive Insights   59

3 Reading for Meaning   **61**

Be Active   61

Stop at Control □'s and Test Understanding   65

Yes, I Do Understand   68

Determine Key Information   68

Identify the Topic   68

Determine the Main Idea   74

Find the Major Supporting Details   82

Predict Test Questions   90

Mark & Highlight Text   91

Continue to the Next □   94

Read to the End of Study Block   95

No, I Don't Understand   95

Use Fix-up Strategies   95

1. Reread   95

2. Read Ahead   96

3. Define Unfamiliar Words   96

4. Read Out Loud   97

5. Mark with "?" to Clear up Later   98

Identify Patterns of Organization   99

Summary   101

Review Questions   102

Metacognitive Insights   103

4 Reducing the Amount to Learn   **105**

Post-View   106

Answer Questions   107

Organize for Recall   108

     Reduction Techniques   109

Make Outlines   110

     How to Make a Successful Outline   112

     Benefits of Outlines   114

Take Notes   115

     How to Take Successful Cornell Notes   116

     General Note-Taking Tips   119

     Benefits of Taking Notes   121

Write Summaries   122

     How to Write a Successful Summary   122

     Benefits of Summaries   124

Create Maps   125

     How to Create a Successful Map   127

     Benefits of Mapping   133

Summary   135

Review Questions   136

Metacognitive Insights   137

5 Retaining the Key Information   **139**

How Your Mind Works   140

     The Sensory Store   141

     Short-Term Memory   141

     Long-Term Memory   142

Teach Someone   143

Study in Groups   145

     Forming Study Groups   146

     Study Group Guidelines   147

Recreate in Writing   148

     Recognition Versus Recall Level Learning   149

     Split-Page Testing   150

Make Study Cards   153

     Advantages of Using Study Cards   156

Use Mnemonics 157

    Rhymes 158

    Acronyms 159

    Acrostics 161

    Mini Stories 163

    Songs 164

    Picture Links 164

    Peg System 166

    Loci Systems 169

Rehearse 173

Summary 175

Review Questions 176

Metacognitive Insights 177

6 Personalizing BICUM **179**

Overview: Four Reading Stages 179

Make Some Modifications 182

Create a Plan that Works for You 185

Your Personalized Study Plan 187

Test-Taking Tips: Prove that You Remember 189

    Test Anxiety 189

    Before the Test 190

    During the Test 193

    After the Test 198

Summary 201

Review Questions 202

Metacognitive Questions 203

Appendix A: Practice Paragraphs **205**

Appendix B: Patterns of Organization **209**

References **215**

PREFACE TO THE INSTRUCTOR

A Unique Approach to Reading Improvement: Metacognition

Taking Control of Your College Reading and Learning is unique. Including both direct instruction and application of reading skills, this book presents a powerful metacognitive reading training program called **BICUM** (**Be In Control: Use Metacognition**). By learning and practicing the material in this book, students not only improve their reading skills, but they also become *aware of their awareness* and gain control over their own learning. As students develop metacognitive awareness, they gather knowledge about themselves, knowledge about the tasks they face, and awareness of and practice in using a variety of study-reading strategies. Armed with this valuable information, students then create personalized reading plans that fit their needs. The independence they gain from mastering these skills empowers them to "become their own best teachers"—that is, they learn to accept the responsibility for their own education.

Taking Control empowers students not just to read for comprehension, but for effective learning techniques as well. In this information age, our students may be required to change occupations several times. Therefore, the most valuable training students can receive is to *learn how to learn*. They need to become independent learners rather than to depend on professors to dispense information. Since reading is fundamental to learning, this textbook trains students to take an active part in their education.

How the Approach Was Developed

After an extensive review of reading research, Elaine Byrd first developed the basic framework for the *Taking Control* approach in 1985, during a summer master's degree internship at Hood College in Frederick, Maryland. Since that time the program has undergone several revisions. Over the past several years, it has been fine-tuned through suggestions from students and colleagues. The present text has been written, expanded, and revisited with the synergistic efforts of Elaine Byrd, Elaine Carter, and Stacy Waddoups. It has been introduced in colleges on the East Coast, as well as in the western United States.

Research Support

Several research studies have shown that use of *Taking Control of Your College Reading and Learning* helps improve student grades. For two years, this book was used as the textbook in a one-credit study-reading course that was paired with a required course called Ethics and Values. Each year a comparison of the final grades showed that students who took the study-reading course scored a half to a full letter grade higher in the Ethics and Values course than students who took the content course without the reading course. These results were found to be statistically significant. (For more specific information, see the dissertation entitled, "Paired College Study-Reading Courses: An Investigation of the Effectiveness of a Reduced Credit Metacognitive Model," by Dr. Elaine H. Byrd, Brigham Young University, Provo, Utah: August 1999)

Currently, *Taking Control of Your College Reading and Learning* is being used in a course pairing between study-reading and general biology. Student grades are again a half to a full letter grade higher for those who are taking the paired reading course that utilizes this book than students who are taking the biology class without the reading class.

Organization and Content

Consisting of six chapters, this book begins by introducing and explaining metacognition.

- Chapter 1 sets up a training program in self-awareness that is reinforced with Metacognitive Training Activities (**MTAs**) throughout the book.

- The next four chapters describe the four basic stages for understanding and remembering what you read: *Ready, Read, Reduce,* and *Retain.* Each of these stages offers a variety of strategies for effective reading, conducting self-inventories, previewing, setting up comprehension testing, and selecting fix-up strategies. Students experiment with each of these as they develop awareness of how their own minds function. Students determine key information such as main ideas and supporting details, along with learning outlining, note taking, summarizing, and mapping. A full chapter on time-proven memory techniques is included.

- The final chapter presents specific guidelines for personalizing **BICUM** to meet individual student's needs and test-taking tips to help students prove they remember the information they have read.

- Finally, in-text references are presented in full in the bibliography at the end of the text.

Key Features

- **Comprehensive and Streamlined Packaging:** With four easy-to-remember stages, Ready, Read, Reduce, and Retain, this plan incorporates a menu of proven study-reading strategies and presents them in a way that students can easily understand and apply.

- **Bookmarks:** Just after the Preface to the Student and at the end of the text are two copies of a bookmark presenting an overview or outline of **BICUM.** The bookmark lists the four study-reading stages: *Ready, Read, Reduce,* and *Retain.* Under each stage, a menu of strategies offers guidelines for successful study-reading. Students can put these bookmarks in their textbooks to remind them of how to study-read effectively.

- **Chapter Overviews:** At the beginning of each chapter is an overview that highlights some of the most important study strategies discussed in that chapter. Recognize that these are not chapter outlines; that is, they do not cover all of the points discussed in the chapters. Chapter 1 overview is a smaller version of the BICUM bookmark, showing all four of the study-reading stages. Chapters 2 through 4 each cover one of the four stages. Chapter 6 overview is a copy of the bookmark without the strategies listed. In this chapter, students create their own study-reading plan specific to their learning styles and needs by filling in strategies they have found work for them. They can then use their personalized programs for future study.

- **The SELF Inventory:** This unique metacognitive strategy listed under the first stage guides students to check their reading readiness. It considers four crucial areas that could influence success in reading:

Study area

Emotion evaluation

Level of difficulty of the material to be read

Feeling physically

After reviewing these areas, students then decide how to modify, eliminate, or at least prepare for possible problems.

- **Control Boxes (☐):** Another key feature of the text is the Control ☐'s. In the Ready stage students are taught how to use the information from their SELF inventories by inserting ☐'s to mark stopping places in their reading assignments. Later, as students read, they stop at each ☐ to assess their understanding, proceeding if they understand or correcting difficulties if they do not. In this way, these ☐'s also serve as "wake-up" calls to help students stay focused.

- **Metacognitive Training Activities (MTAs):** Located throughout the book, MTAs are carefully constructed assignments designed to help students develop self-awareness. By completing these activities, students will begin to notice the unique way that they perceive and process information. They will gradually become "experts" in knowing what strategies work best for them. Students are encouraged to keep a journal and/or respond to the Metacognitive Insights at the end of each chapter to record the information they learn about themselves during these activities.

- **Option to Personalize the Program:** Personalizing **BICUM** gives students ongoing control to choose and adapt strategies that meet their personal situations, learning styles, and various reading tasks. This is one of the most appealing parts of this study-reading program because personalization lowers the complacency or boredom that often occurs when students must repeatedly follow preset steps.

- **Margin Boxes:** The crucial information in each chapter is highlighted through the use of margin boxes to make the key ideas more accessible to the students.

- **Appendixes:** Appendix A contains paragraphs that students may use to practice identifying topics, main ideas, and major supporting details. By using uniform textbook material for practice, instructors can more quickly help students master these important skills. Appendix B contains a chart showing several patterns of organization frequently used in textbooks. It also has a discussion of each pattern and examples to illustrate each one.

- **Teachers' Manual:** This valuable tool contains suggestions for implementing the study-reading program, course syllabi, teaching tips, answers to chapter questions, test bank of exams, and students' responses to the program.

Ways to Use This Text

Companion Textbook for Developmental Reading: Many textbooks for college reading courses offer direct instruction in reading skills and a wide variety of academic readings, but they do not contain a plan for putting those skills into action. *Taking Control of Your College Reading and Learning* helps fill this gap because it presents a study-reading plan that trains students how to immediately apply what they are learning. This text has been used successfully with several popular reading texts. The authors have found that combining this text with another traditional reading text offers a practical and more complete instruction package for students.

Supplementary Textbook for College Success: Because college success textbooks often devote only minimal attention to reading instruction, our book works well as a supplement to these texts. Also, because the focus is on learning how to learn, students often independently apply their improved reading skills to their other college classes.

Paired Courses: Pairing reading classes with required general education courses is known to be a particularly effective method of teaching college reading skills. When reading courses are linked to content courses, applying newly learned skills takes on greater relevance. This text is an excellent book for such a course combination. One of the strengths of this program is its streamlined approach to reading instruction. The authors have found that *Taking Control of Your College Reading and Learning* can successfully be taught in a one credit study-reading class that is paired with other content courses. We have used this book for pairing study-reading courses with biology and with philosophy. Data from these pairings consistently shows that students in paired content sections earn a half to a full letter grade higher in the content classes than students in the non-paired sections. The power of this combination is twofold. First, the pairing helps students develop study-reading skills so they can stay in courses and successfully complete them, and second, the content course material serves as a vehicle to teach transferable study-reading skills that can be applied immediately and also used in future college classes.

Student Profile

A wide variety of students can benefit from learning and applying the strategies contained in this text. This book has been used successfully by scholarship students; developmental and international students; older, returning students; and in-coming freshmen. Although their needs and textbook challenges may vary, students respond to the principles in much the same way; they all learn to take control of their college reading. They are energized and empowered by the choices available in this text for understanding and remembering what they read.

PREFACE TO THE STUDENT

Do you dread reading textbook reading assignments?

Does your mind wander?

Do you daydream or even fall asleep while trying to read a textbook chapter? Even worse, when you finish an assignment, do you forget what you have read?

If you have experienced any of these situations, you are not alone. These are very common occurrences. Since reading textbooks requires specific skills that usually are not taught in high school, many college students are unprepared for the difficult tasks involved in college level reading. Fortunately, you can improve your academic effectiveness by learning and using an effective study system. *Taking Control of Your College Reading and Learning* presents a streamlined study-reading program referred to by the acronym **BICUM: B**e **I**n **C**ontrol: **U**se **M**etacognition. This system is designed specifically for busy college students who want to be more effective in understanding and remembering material from textbooks. Consisting of four stages, each with several strategies, BICUM trains you to transfer material from textbooks to your memory. Following this study system can change your frustration with textbooks into enthusiasm for learning.

As you read through the chapters of this book, you will see the names of authors whose ideas are important to a particular discussion. Some of these works are very technical; some are not. If you want to investigate the writing of any author listed, you will find the complete information about the book or article in the References at the end of this book.

Instructions for removing and folding
BICUM bookmarks

·⌒·

Cut out one of your bookmarks along the dashed line. Fold
in half along the center black line so that the four panels are
on the inside. Then fold in half again lengthwise. The word
BICUM should be on the front panel of your bookmark.

Retain

- Teach Someone
- Study in Groups
- Recreate in Writing
- Make Study Cards
- Use Mnemonics
- Rehearse

Reduce

- Post View
- Answer Questions
- Organize for Recall

(Select 1)

- make outlines
- take notes
- write summaries
- create maps

Read

- Be Active
- Stop at ☐'s and Test Understanding

Yes, I do understand

No, I don't understand

- Use fix-up strategies
  1. Reread
  2. Read ahead
  3. Define unfamiliar words
  4. Read out loud
  5. Mark with "?" to clear up later

- Determine key information
- Predict test questions
- Mark & highlight text

Continue to next ☐

get Ready

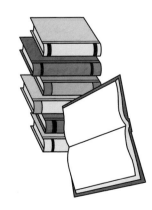

- Inventory **SELF**
  Study area
  Emotions
  Level of difficulty
  Feeling physically

- Preview
- Select or Create Questions
- Set Study Length
- Place Control ☐'s

Taking Control
of Your College
Reading

●●●●●●●●●●

4 *R*'s for
Remembering
What You Read:

Ready
Read
Reduce
Retain

Be In Control
Use Metacognition
BICUM

ACKNOWLEDGMENTS

We are grateful to the many colleagues, students, and friends who have given us the help and encouragement necessary to develop and improve *Taking Control of Your College Reading and Learning*. Elaine Byrd wishes to thank Dr. Beth Ann Herrmann for her guidance in the initial stages of **BICUM** study-reading and for her friendship and encouragement over the past years.

A special thanks to our families for putting up with deadlines, late nights and early mornings, and for taking care of the home front. Without their encouragement and support, this book would not have been possible.

We owe our colleagues a debt of gratitude for their ideas and steadfast belief in this project. Peggy Pasin was a major driving force behind this publication. Her insistence that this book be written, her numerous suggestions for improvements, and her belief in these concepts have given us the courage to move forward. We also are indebted to Mari Beth Ivie and Annette Hill for their useful suggestions. We thank Eldon McMurray for his insightful additions to such strategies as Control □'s, Double Question Q-Cards, and the philosophy of training students to become their own best teachers. These have improved the effectiveness of this study-reading program. We thank Dr. Grant Richards for his support and Kathryn Hall for her editorial expertise with an eye for detail. We appreciate the support staff in the Learning Enrichment Center for their essential computer and secretarial assistance and for their patience and sense of humor.

Contributions from students and tutors are greatly appreciated. Insights we gained from students helped us view the material from a different perspective. We acknowledge the suggestions and insights of the many students and teachers who have learned and applied the steps and strategies in this program. Their metacognitive comments and recommendations have helped shape this textbook.

We appreciate the vision and excellent editorial support of Kim A. Johnson, Senior Editor for Developmental Education at Wadsworth, with whom the book was originally contracted. She has made valuable suggestions that have been incorporated into this text. We also give credit to the following reviewers for their experienced opinions: Acquanetta L. Bracy, Alabama State University; Patricia Byrne, Camden County College; Anne Elizabeth Gottsdanker, Antelope Valley College; Leslie K. King, State University of New York—Oswego; and Patricia L. Rottmund, Harrisburg Area Community College.

get *Ready*

- Inventory **SELF**
  Study area
  Emotions
  Level of difficulty
  Feeling physically

- Preview

- Select or Create
  Questions

- Set Study Length

- Place Control ❏'s

Read

- Be Active
- Stop at ❏'s and
  Test Understanding

Yes, I do understand | **No**, I don't understand

Yes, I do understand
- Determine key information

- Predict test questions

- Mark & highlight text

No, I don't understand
- Use fix-up strategies
  1. Reread
  2. Read ahead
  3. Define unfamiliar words
  4. Read out loud
  5. Mark with "?" to clear up later

Continue to next ❏

Overview
Four Stages of Reading

Reduce

- Post View

- Answer
  Questions

- Organize for
  Recall

(Select 1)

– make outlines

– take notes

– write summaries

– create maps

Retain

- Teach
  Someone

- Study in
  Groups

- Recreate in
  Writing

- Make Study
  Cards

- Use
  Mnemonics

- Rehearse

TAKING CONTROL OF YOUR READING

Why can't I understand and remember what I read?

Why does it take me so long to finish text assignments?

Why is it so difficult for me to concentrate while reading?

Do you ever have questions like the ones above? Although these concerns are common among students entering college, many freshmen find them surprising because they view themselves as good readers. Actually, most college students are capable readers; they have no problem with everyday reading of newspapers and magazines or enjoying an occasional novel.

High School Versus College Reading

Reading college textbooks requires a distinctly different set of skills than casual reading, and high school students are not usually taught how to read college level material. In fact, many students report that they did not have to read textbooks in order to do well in their high school classes. They could get by simply by memorizing handouts in order to be prepared for tests. With no textbook reading instruction and but little practice, it is no wonder that many otherwise very capable freshmen struggle when they are faced with the complex textbook reading assignments required by many college professors.

Understanding textbooks involves much more than just reading words. Most beginning college students think that when they are finished reading, they have completed their assignments and are through studying. However, this approach can be disastrous, because about 80 percent of what one reads and understands will be forgotten within 24 hours. Therefore the academic tasks assigned in college require effort before, during, and after reading in order for comprehension and retention to take place. In fact, effective college reading demands focused *study-reading,* a conscious combination of thinking, reasoning, and controlling learning through deliberate choices. An overview of effective reading and retention strategies is given on the beginning page of this chapter. Each of these panels will be discussed in the chapters that follow.

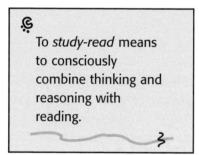

To *study-read* means to consciously combine thinking and reasoning with reading.

Study-Reading

Study-reading is best done by using an organized approach. Educators and researchers have long recognized the need for study systems, and through the years many such approaches have been developed. Francis P. Robinson was one of the pioneers in developing a system for study. His ideas laid the foundation for many programs that followed.

Many students search for ways to improve their effectiveness and are willing to try techniques they believe will work for them with their particular learning style. Since all students learn differently, "the key to any [study] system's effectiveness may very well lie in how students learn to control their reading through selective and flexible use. A [study] system evolves gradually within each learner" (Vacca and Vacca 1989). Since most college students are pushed for time, they are only willing to use methods that actually reduce their study time and increase their test scores. They do not make time for activities they view as busy work.

The authors of this textbook agree with these researchers; the key to effective study-reading systems is in their flexibility so they can be appropriately modified and adapted by individual students. The study system presented in this textbook is specifically designed to be changed, "to evolve over time" to meet students' specific needs.

Furthermore, this textbook specifically trains you in self-awareness so that you can consciously make modifications and adaptions that meet your individual needs.

In the final chapter of this book, you will be asked to create your own personalized study-reading program. You will be prepared to do this because you will have gathered valuable knowledge about yourself while completing the exercises in the earlier chapters. Using this information, you will identify specific study-reading techniques that work for you. You will then organize these strategies into a meaningful study system, one that is "tailor-made" to fit your needs. Thousands of students who have used this personalized approach report that they continue to use their study-reading systems long after they initially create them.

Interactive Reading

Several research studies, including the one by Paris and Turner (1991), have indicated that conscious, active involvement in reading is perhaps the most distinguishing factor between expert and novice readers. Their research clearly documents that some readers do not know how to actively monitor their reading. They do not understand that reading is intended to be an interactive process where a type of conversation is taking place between the reader and the author. Instead, many readers concentrate so much on pronouncing the words and understanding the individual definitions that they lose track of the author's message.

It is important to recognize comprehension problems while reading and to intentionally employ strategies to clear up confusion. If you view reading as a sense-making process, then you can become an intentional, independent learner. By making a conscience effort to employ the skills presented in this text, anyone can improve his or her reading ability. Many of the thought processes needed to become an expert reader are contained in the concept known as *metacognition*.

Reading is an interactive process between reader and author.

Developing Metacognition

Metacognition is a word probably unfamiliar to you because it is not found in a standard dictionary. It was first coined by J.H. Flavell in mid-1970. Notice that the first part of the word metacognition is "meta." This is a Greek prefix meaning *beyond, transcending* or *more comprehensive.* "Meta" as it relates to learning means self-awareness. The last part of the word, "cognition," refers to perception or mental processing. A simplistic definition of metacognition is an awareness of how your mind processes information.

Actually, the concept of metacognition includes more than just knowing about how you think. Craig (1998) and Palincsar and Brown (1987) agree with many other researchers when they characterize metacognition as having two distinct, yet related parts: (1) awareness of one's thinking, and (2) regulation of one's cognitive processes. Therefore, a more complete definition of metacognition includes both an awareness of how one learns and a conscious regulation of the process. The value of metacognition for students lies in its use to regulate or direct learning. Expert readers instinctively guide their reading and learning, but those who are less aware can also develop these skills. Carefully consider the following overview of metacognition.

Metacognition is the procedure of actively investigating how your mind works. It is monitoring how well you understand what you read, recognizing comprehension breakdowns, exploring possible fix-up strategies, and then implementing corrective measures. It is awareness of the assignments you face and deciding what strategies will best help you complete your academic tasks. Metacognition is actively monitoring or thinking about your thinking as you read and learn.

It is your responsibility to manage your learning (Blakey & Spence 1990). This involves connecting new information to what you already know, deliberately selecting thinking strategies, then planning, observing and evaluating your thinking as you proceed through your reading assignments.

For example, if you used metacognition when reading a biology textbook assignment, you would consciously prepare

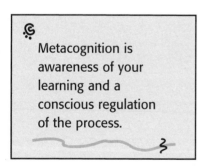

Metacognition is awareness of your learning and a conscious regulation of the process.

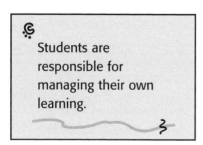

Students are responsible for managing their own learning.

yourself both mentally and physically to read effectively. Then you would begin reading the material, actively searching for meaning and organizing the information in your mind as you moved through the text. When the words did not make sense or the ideas did not fit together to make meaningful units, you would recognize the problem. You would then use one or more fix-up strategies (discussed in detail in Chapter 3) to get back on track, e.g., rereading, reading ahead, or defining unknown words. You would notice if your mind began to wander. In short, you would *know about your knowing and consciously evaluate and regulate your learning.* Can you see that by reading with this focused self-perception, you would learn much more from textbooks than you would if you let your mind wander?

Metacognitive Training

Some students use metacognition naturally, but it can also be learned. Research repeatedly confirms that metacognition can be taught. However, developing metacognitive skills does not happen in one training session; it is an ongoing process. It is a skill that improves with practice. As you acquire self-knowledge and experiment with a variety of reading and study strategies, your metacognitive skill will expand.

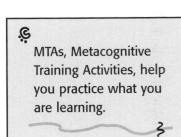

MTAs, Metacognitive Training Activities, help you practice what you are learning.

Throughout this book, you will find a variety of Metacognitive Training Activities (**MTAs**). These are exercises designed to practice the many strategies you will be learning. MTAs will help you gather information about yourself as a reader and about the textbooks you are reading. Since much of what is involved in completing and reporting on the MTAs is subjective and difficult to measure from simply looking at your written responses, you will be asked to self-grade your success in completing each MTA and then justify your grade with one or more sentences of back-up.

Your grade should be based on several considerations. First, it will be important to assess the quality of your effort in completing each MTA. Second, you will need to decide whether you used the techniques or strategies correctly. Third, your grade should also reflect how clearly and completely you answered every question. Self assessment is always difficult, but it is also a necessary part of taking control of your own learning.

Since your instructor has the ultimate responsibility of assigning your course grade, she/he will make the final decision on what grade you should receive on each MTA. If you want your instructor to take your self-grades seriously, it is important to show honesty and maturity in not only completing MTAs but also in grading them. If the instructor does not agree with your grade, it will be his/her responsibility to explain why.

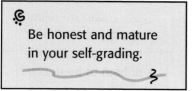

Be honest and mature in your self-grading.

Since the instructor has more experience than you do and can compare your assignment to those of other students, it will clearly be easier for her/him to determine if the grade you have given yourself is fair and accurate. With practice and good feed-back from your instructor, this self-grading process should become easier for you over time.

Recognize that you do not have to complete the MTAs precisely when or where they are introduced in the text. Rather, complete the MTAs when your teacher assigns them or when they would be most helpful to you. Also, recognize that repeating these activities can be useful because each time you perform them, you will reaffirm or discover valuable information about yourself. Remember, MTAs will help you develop control over your learning.

Since each student is unique, it is necessary that you collect a personal set of data about your thinking and learning processes as you study-read textbooks. Record the information on the "Metacognitive Insights" pages located at the end of each chapter. You will need this information in Chapter 6, when you create your personal version of **BICUM.** You may be asked to create your own bookmark, one that contains the techniques and strategies you have found to work best for you. In order to determine which methods are most effective, it will of course be necessary to try as many of them as possible. At the end of the semester, some instructors will ask you to summarize the information you learn about yourself, your academic tasks, and your favorite strategies in a portfolio.

The following MTA is designed to help you assess how much you already know about yourself and the way that

METACOGNITIVE TRAINING ACTIVITY
Metacognitive Preassessment
·⁊· MTA 1.1 ·⁊·

⅗ DIRECTIONS:

A good way to begin metacognitive training is to assess how much
you already know about your thinking. Honestly answering the
following questions will start you on the path to self-awareness.

Put the title and number of this MTA at the top of your paper.

Number each of your responses for ease in grading.

Word your answers carefully to clearly communicate what you are
trying to say.

1. a. What type of material is easiest for you to read? Why?

   b. How do you remember it?

2. a. What type of material is hardest for you to read? Why?

   b. How is remembering this type of material different from
   remembering easier material?

3. What do you do to get ready to read?

4. a. What causes you to lose concentration when reading?

   b. What do you usually do when you realize that you have not
   been concentrating?

5. Name one thing that you can do if you recognize that you are
   not understanding what you are reading.

6. Do you try to predict test questions from your reading? Why or
   why not?

7. Self grade _____% and brief justification. (Please give yourself
   a percentage grade on this assignment; see guidelines on p. 6.)
   Justify your grade, or tell why you believe that you have earned
   that score.

your mind processes information. It will also help you look at academic tasks and discover what learning methods you may already be using while reading college textbooks.

Self-, Task-, and Strategy-Awareness

According to El-Hindi (1992), psychologists and educators alike have repeatedly confirmed that awareness of cognitive processes is correlated with reading. Ruth Garner (1994) further clarified the significance of metacognition by dividing cognitive awareness into three main areas: knowledge about *oneself,* knowledge about the *tasks* one faces, and knowledge about the *strategies* to employ. The following will help you to understand the three types of awareness needed in metacognition:

- self-awareness
- task-awareness
- strategy-awareness

However, in her division of metacognition, Garner did not intend that these three parts be viewed as independent of each other. The division was only for clarification. Sometimes viewing the individual components of a concept can facilitate understanding and utilization of the information. In practice, all three areas of metacognitive awareness are interrelated. Wellman (1983) emphasizes this point when he describes metacognitive knowledge as "an intricately interwoven system of knowledge." Metacognition incorporates all three kinds of awareness.

Self-, task-, and strategy-awareness help you discover what you need to do in order to read, understand, remember, and then retrieve information. You need all three components of metacognition to successfully extract material from a textbook and eventually store that information in your mind in an organized manner so you can successfully retrieve it when needed. Following is a discussion of each of these three types of awareness.

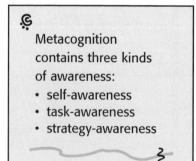

Metacognition contains three kinds of awareness:
- self-awareness
- task-awareness
- strategy-awareness

Self-Awareness

Metacognitive self-awareness is what you know or believe about yourself. It is identifying your strengths and weaknesses as a learner and collecting information about what it takes for you to be a successful student. Each person has a unique set of academic strengths and weaknesses. No two people learn in exactly the same way.

A personalized list of information about how your brain works is indispensable to construct a learning program that fits your needs and the specific academic tasks you face. Since you live with yourself 24 hours a day, you are the perfect person to compile such a list. Metacognitive self-awareness is consciously observing yourself in learning tasks and noting what works for you and what does not. Examples of this component of metacognition include insights such as the following:

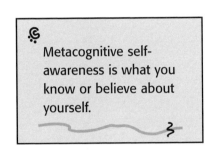

Metacognitive self-awareness is what you know or believe about yourself.

> I have more difficulty focusing when I read history than when I read biology.
>
> I fall asleep when I study after ten o'clock at night.
>
> Mathematics is easy for me; I enjoy working with numbers.

DISTRACTIONS: EXTERNAL AND INTERNAL   Physical, mental, emotional, and environmental conditions can effect your reading; observe these conditions as you read. You can then use this knowledge to make appropriate adjustments before, during, or after you read. The following questions might help you begin to generate self-awareness information:

> Is my study environment conducive to learning?
>
> What physical, mental, or emotional changes are needed to optimize my learning?
>
> Is the time of day appropriate for me and for the type of study I'm doing?
>
> How motivated am I?
>
> How much resistance or anxiety does this task generate for me?

By asking yourself these kinds of questions, your self-awareness will increase. You will start to learn about your own learning and how to consciously impact the process.

CONCENTRATION   Many students can verify that it is possible to be present physically but not mentally when reading textbooks. It is a lot more difficult to read textbooks than to read magazines, newspapers, or novels. If you are not interested in a subject, staying focused while reading can be challenging. If you consistently have difficulty concentrating on your reading assignments, you are missing important material.

Fortunately, you can train yourself to stay focused. Concentration is a skill that can be developed. Instead of leisurely reading textbooks, you need to learn to study-read. You can learn to be aware of your thoughts and deliberately direct your attention to your reading. This means that your mind is aware of what you are doing and that you are consciously experiencing the present. You are not dwelling on past events or worrying about future responsibilities and, as a result, missing out on the significance of the present. You are tuning in to the "now" and using your energies to make the most of each moment.

Start to expand your self-awareness by consciously focusing the next time you begin a reading assignment. If you sincerely concentrate on the author's message, you will see a dramatic improvement in your reading skills as you really engage in what the author is saying. However, if you are like most people, you will likely be surprised at how often your mind wanders while you are reading.

By using focused concentration to stay alert during reading assignments, you will use your energy to concentrate completely on the information being presented. This can increase your chances of understanding and remembering what you have read. Look for information you think will be interesting. Decide to clear up any ideas or concepts that are confusing.

STAYING FOCUSED   While you are reading, if your mind begins to wander, try to identify every cause. Notice whether the distraction is something external in your environment, such as noise, people, or poor lighting. Perhaps the distraction is internal, such as worries or daydreaming. By

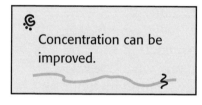

Concentration can be improved.

noticing every cause, your chances of overcoming distractions are greatly increased. Once you are aware of factors that affect your study-reading, you can then remind yourself of your commitment to stay focused.

Do not be discouraged if you experience setbacks as you try to stay focused. All readers lose focus from time to time. Fortunately, with continued practice and increased awareness, most readers will see marked improvement in their concentration. The chapters that follow contain a number of effective techniques for improving your concentration and comprehension.

Task-Awareness

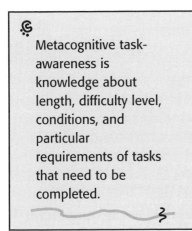

Metacognitive task-awareness is knowledge about length, difficulty level, conditions, and particular requirements of tasks that need to be completed.

After reviewing the factors that affect your self-awareness, consider task-awareness. Metacognitive task-awareness is knowledge about the length, difficulty level, conditions, and particular requirements of tasks that need to be completed. College textbook reading offers special task-awareness challenges for a number of reasons. Not only do these texts contain more difficult vocabulary, but some ordinary words are used in unique ways. Also, there are often numerous ideas in a single sentence. When many difficult, new words are contained in one sentence or paragraph, the level of reading difficulty increases.

The more you know about the task(s) ahead, the more likely you are to choose effective strategies to complete them. For example, sometimes the length of the reading assignment is discouraging, intimidating, or both. In this case, your awareness of the task will help you divide the reading into manageable chunks.

Another aspect of task-awareness is understanding how ideas in sentences and paragraphs work together in specific ways to convey meaning. Chapter 3 will help you improve in this area of task-awareness. As the consciousness of these relationships increases, you will gain greater control over the reading process. Other examples of metacognitive task-awareness follow:

Reading is an interactive process between reader and author.

> My task is to organize the important information from my psychology chapter so I can be prepared for the test.

I need to find the answers to the chapter questions.

My task is to read my history textbook so that I will be able to discuss it in class.

Strategy-Awareness

Metacognitive strategy-awareness combines knowledge of the content of the chapter with an understanding of how to use a variety of procedures and control strategies. It also involves knowing *when* and *where* to use these strategies. Examples of this awareness include statements such as the following:

Reading out loud helps me understand confusing textbook passages.

I remember information better when I study in groups.

My underlining is more meaningful if I wait to underline until after I have finished reading a section.

These insights can help you know if the strategies you chose are effective. Strategy-awareness is the major focus of this text. This book is a menu of study-reading tools. It presents and provides practice and application for a wide variety of time-tested strategies. By using these strategies, you can significantly reduce study time and may increase learning and test scores. The remainder of the book contains easy-to-read explanations of many strategies that can be implemented immediately in any study-reading task.

The following MTA is designed to help you evaluate all three components of metacognitive awareness: self-, task-, and strategy-awareness. Completing this MTA should help prepare you for the more in-depth metacognitive activities that will be presented in later chapters.

Believing in Yourself: Self-Efficacy

As you develop metacognitive skills, your overall self-confidence will increase. Referred to by researchers as *self-efficacy* (the degree to which you believe you can succeed),

METACOGNITIVE TRAINING ACTIVITY
Cognitive Awareness
·୧· MTA 1.2 ·୧·

⅂ DIRECTIONS:

Select a reading assignment from one of your college courses to evaluate your readiness to read.

Before you begin your reading assignment, look over the numbered items below so that you will know how to respond when you finish the assignment.

Respond to the following items by number. Remember to also put the title and number of the MTA at the top of your paper.

Self-Awareness:

1. Record the course, text, and chapter title.

2. List two mental, physical, or emotional distractions that you will need to overcome to read the assignment effectively.

3. Record the place where you are now studying.

4. Is your study environment conducive to learning? Why or why not?

5. Is the time of day optimum for you and for the type of studying being done? Explain.

Task-Awareness:

6. How long is this assignment? List the total number of pages.

7. Record how much time you predict it will take you to read this assignment. Time yourself, and record whether your prediction was accurate or not.

8. How difficult does this assignment appear to be (based on such things as vocabulary, subject matter, or interest level).

Strategy-Awareness:

9. If the reading becomes difficult or if your mind starts to wander, what techniques could you use to stay focused?

10. Self grade _____% and brief justification.

self-confidence can be a decisive factor in your college achievement. Bandura (1986) and Weiner (1986), among other researchers, have confirmed the relationship between self-efficacy and student performance. Students with high levels of self-efficacy perform better than students who doubt their abilities.

An important part of high self-efficacy is positive *self-talk*, or messages that we silently say to ourselves. Twenty-three hours a day, the human mind engages in self-talk. Researchers believe that, except for approximately one hour during the deepest part of the sleep cycle, when no self-talk occurs, the mind is actively talking to itself. Both the conscious and subconscious minds consistently deliver messages to the brain, and the brain accepts what it is told. The subconscious mind does not distinguish between what is real and what is unreal (Christensen 1995).

The content of this internal dialogue has enormous educational significance. You are the essence of what you think about most. When the mind receives skeptical, negative thoughts, it promotes this agenda. When the mind receives constructive, positive messages, it likewise promotes these thoughts. In a real sense, who you are today is the result of yesterdays' thoughts.

Since personal thoughts have such far-reaching effects in your life, it is important to consider where these thoughts come from and to what extent they can be programmed or changed. There seems to be some consensus among the experts that self-talk can be changed and directed.

Likewise experts agree that students can learn to construct success scripts to help them surmount academic obstacles. Use of positive self-talk such as, "I can do this," "I am capable," or "I am improving everyday" can encourage academic success.

If you are like many people, you often think negative thoughts. Some researchers, including Christensen (1995), speculate that nearly seventy percent of self-talk is negative. However, you can make changes. You do not have to continue simply reacting to your environment or accepting what you or others have programmed your brain to follow. You have the power to control your thoughts, and as a result, you have the power to control your actions.

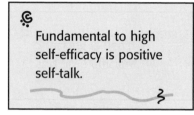

Fundamental to high self-efficacy is positive self-talk.

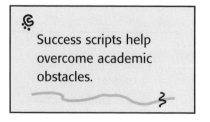

Success scripts help overcome academic obstacles.

Recognize that all actions are created mentally before they are performed physically (Covey 1989). First, thoughts are created in the mind, and second, thoughts are turned into actions. Buildings and bridges are first conceived in the architects' thoughts before they are constructed physically. Music is first played in the composer's mind before it is written and performed. And students first think about succeeding in college long before they begin to perform the necessary actions of reading, studying, and test taking that make their college success dreams a reality.

Student responsibility is fundamental to high self-efficacy and positive internal dialogue. If you believe in yourself and use positive self-talk, you will accept obligations and responsibilities more easily. Likewise, metacognitive training encourages you to take control of your learning and accept an executive role in the direction of your education. You will find that as you increase your self-awareness, you will begin to let go of the typical self-defeating expressions such as,

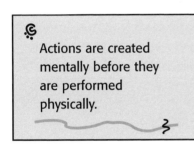

Actions are created mentally before they are performed physically.

> "I can't read that biology textbook; it is boring."

> "I failed the test because the questions were tricky."

> "My roommates kept me talking so I couldn't study."

You will learn to monitor your mind for negative self-talk and then to replace it with language such as,

> "I can read this biology textbook even if I do not naturally find it interesting."

> "I did poorly on the test, but I am going to find out what I missed so I won't repeat the same mistakes again."

> "I realize that I do not study effectively in my apartment when my roommates are talking, so I will go to the library where I can focus more easily."

Can you see how this type of positive self-talk leads to productive, successful actions?

High self-efficacy, positive self-talk, and acceptance of responsibility for one's education are characteristic of metacognitive, expert readers; they are characteristic of independent self-learners who are capable of success in college, in the work place, and in everyday life. This is the kind of reader you may become if you carefully follow the guidelines described in this book.

A Study-Reading Plan

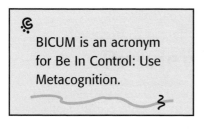

BICUM is an acronym for Be In Control: Use Metacognition.

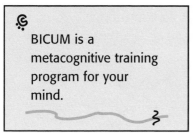

BICUM is a metacognitive training program for your mind.

The study-reading plan used in this book is called **BICUM** (pronounced bîkum), which is an acronym for **Be In Control: Use Metacognition.** The word *metacognition* is mentioned to remind you to continuously monitor your understanding and direct your learning. This acronym is used throughout the rest of the text as an easy way to refer to the stages and strategies presented in this study-reading program.

Keep in mind that BICUM is a metacognitive training program for your mind. It is a plan that guides you to monitor your thinking and to notice which comprehension and memory techniques work for you. As you begin to recognize how your mind gathers and stores data, you can then use this information to control not only your reading but also your learning in other areas.

Developing metacognition in reading requires both discipline and direction. Following a plan that guides you to regularly monitor your reading and thinking will help you develop self-, task-, and strategy-awareness more quickly and more permanently. The four stages of BICUM will provide such a plan.

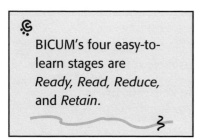

BICUM's four easy-to-learn stages are *Ready, Read, Reduce,* and *Retain*.

The Four Stages in BICUM

BICUM has four easy-to-learn stages:

1. *Ready*—steps to take before you read

2. *Read*—methods for gaining understanding while reading

3. *Reduce*—how to select and condense essential information

   4. *Retain*—ways to remember what you read

   1. *Ready:* In the *Ready* stage you will learn several
       useful strategies that prepare you to understand the
       material you will be reading. By using these
       techniques you will discover metacognitive
       knowledge about yourself and about the tasks you
       will be facing.

   2. *Read:* The *Read* stage will guide you to actively
       search for meaning as you move through your
       textbook chapters. You will learn to pause and test
       your understanding. As you evaluate your
       effectiveness, you may detect comprehension
       problems. If so, you may then select specific fix-up
       strategies designed to clear up confusion. You will
       also learn what information is key to understanding
       and what is not.

   3. *Reduce:* Once you have read your assignment, you
       will learn several ways to condense textbook
       material to only the most important ideas. These
       strategies are covered in the *Reduce* stage. The
       reduction methods in this stage can save you a
       significant amount of time. If you learn and apply
       these methods early, when test dates are announced,
       you will need to study only your reduced forms of
       the text chapters instead of going over complete
       chapters. Rereading text chapters will simply not be
       necessary for you.

   4. *Retain:* The last stage, *Retain,* includes a collection
       of time-proven memory techniques for holding onto
       crucial information.

Benefits of Using BICUM

   Metacognition is key to maximizing reading
effectiveness. As your metacognitive skill increases, you will
develop the ability to direct your thinking. Awareness of
your own specific cognitive resources, skill in the use of a
variety of strategies, and information about the tasks you

Consistent application of the study-reading strategies is key to becoming an expert reader.

face will empower you with tools to guide your learning. Actively regulating your study sessions will expand your learning capabilities and increase the value of your study time.

If you consistently practice using the strategies in the four stages of this program, expect a significant increase in your retention of information. Effective study improves long-term memory. Because you create your own personal study-reading program, it will uniquely match your learning needs, so you might very well notice an increased comfort when studying. In time this comfort will translate into an overall improvement in your attitude about learning. Then, as you encounter challenging college textbook reading assignments, you can confidently use your personalized version of BICUM to take control of your educational success.

Each stage of this program, *Ready, Read, Reduce,* and *Retain* has a menu of strategies or techniques from which to choose. At first, while learning the plan, it is important to try each of the strategies and to consciously notice how your mind responds to them. After several practice sessions in applying the ideas in BICUM, you will begin to see obvious improvements in your reading comprehension as did the following students using this plan.

> The concepts in this text can help anyone be more efficient and effective in college.
>
> —Sue Blain

> I have learned to quickly pull out the key information and to monitor my understanding so I can do something about it.
>
> —Judy Conrad

> Being the mother of four, my time is very limited. These study-reading strategies have taught me what to study and how to do it. I spend much less time doing homework and I can remember what I have learned because it is organized.
>
> —Debbie Thoman

Recognize that when you are learning the stages and strategies of BICUM, you may spend more time completing an assignment. However, once you learn the plan, you will be able to complete your homework more quickly. For example, you will not have to spend long hours rereading in preparation for tests. Instead, you will find that you have learned what to study, and because you have reduced the amount to learn, your retention of the information is much better. Consequently, studying for tests will take less time, and you will likely make better grades as you focus more intently on key information and use more effective retention techniques.

Personalize BICUM

Personalize the BICUM strategies to match your reading tasks.

After you have tried all the strategies listed in the plan, you should personalize BICUM to fit your academic tasks. (Personalizing this study-reading plan is discussed in depth in Chapter 6.) Continue to use the strategies that work for you, but omit any that you do not need. You may also add additional strategies if you find others that are effective. Actually, you can adjust the plan any time you sit down to study. Remember to consider the purpose of your study, what you hope to accomplish, the kind of material you are reading, and the amount of time available to spend on the assignment. Then select the strategies that best meet your needs.

For example, when all you need is a general overview of the material, just preview and read the introduction, summary, and bold print. Sometimes, when you need to know most of the information, but only have a short time to spend on the assignment, just use the first two stages in BICUM: *Ready* and *Read*. In other situations, when a high level of retention is required, and you have wisely allotted sufficient study time, you should follow all of the strategies that are helpful to you. Each time you study, use what you need to be successful. Keep in mind that this plan is designed for efficiency. Your goal should be to study-read as quickly as possible and to remember what you read.

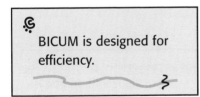

BICUM is designed for efficiency.

Conversely, don't feel that you have to alter any of the suggested strategies to make the plan yours. Many students are very successful using this study system exactly as it is written. As you develop your self-, task-, and strategy-awareness, your learning capacity will increase. This information will place you in the best position to decide what to include or what leave out. You will be in control of your reading.

Summary

Reading college textbooks requires a different set of skills than is needed for everyday reading. Study-reading, a conscious combining of thinking and reasoning with reading, is needed for successful understanding of these challenging materials.

Researchers have identified several differences between expert and novice readers. Some have suggested that the most distinguishing characteristic between these two groups is the degree to which they are involved in their reading. Studies show that expert readers use metacognition, awareness of and control of one's learning, more often than novice readers. Metacognition can be divided into three main areas, self-awareness, task-awareness, and strategy-awareness. Researchers seem to agree that metacognitive skills can be learned by those who do not naturally have these abilities.

Self-efficacy, the degree to which students believe they can succeed, is a major factor in college success. Developing metacognitive skills helps students gain this confidence. When metacognition is combined with positive self-talk and acceptance of responsibility, students can effectively take control of their education.

The study-reading plan presented in this book is BICUM, (Be In Control: Use Metacognition). The four stages in this plan are *Ready, Read, Reduce,* and *Retain*. It would be helpful if you would experiment with all of the strategies listed under each of these stages. As you use the strategies, notice which ones fit your learning needs. Then you can personalize this plan, omitting strategies that are not useful to you and adding additional ones you find helpful. The next four chapters cover each of the four stages in this study-reading program.

Be serious about learning and practicing BICUM. Remember, following this study system can change frustration with textbooks into enthusiasm for learning.

Review Questions

1. According to the experts, what are some of the essential components of interactive reading?

2. What does metacognition mean? How can it help you to take control of your college reading?

3. What three areas of awareness are included in metacognition? How can knowing about these be helpful?

4. What is self-efficacy, and how does it affect student performance? Give three personal examples of how you could change negative thoughts to positive thoughts.

5. Explain two ways you can improve concentration if your mind begins to wander while reading a text assignment.

6. What does the acronym **BICUM** stand for?

7. What are the four major stages (or the 4 Rs) of the BICUM study-reading program? Name two of the stages you believe you need most, and tell why you chose them.

8. What is the purpose of completing the **MTAs**?

9. Since using BICUM sometimes requires more time for students to complete assignments, why would they still want to use this study-reading system? Explain.

10. What does it mean to personalize BICUM? Why is this an important thing to do?

Metacognitive Insights

As your cognitive awareness increases, you will begin to notice important ideas about how you read and how you learn. It is a good idea to record this information. You will need these ideas when you create your personalized version of BICUM in Chapter 6. Begin by responding to the following items. Use the remaining lines to write additional information as you gain new metacognitive insights.

1. What did you learn from completing the MTAs in Chapter 1? _____
_____
_____
_____
_____
_____

2. How easy or difficult was it for you to remain focused while reading? Explain.
_____
_____

3. How will metacognition help you as a learner? _____
_____
_____

4. Which one of the three kinds of cognitive awareness do you need the most? Explain.
_____
_____

ADDITIONAL INSIGHTS

_____
_____
_____
_____
_____
_____

get *Ready*

- Inventory **SELF**
  Study area
  Emotions
  Level of difficulty
  Feeling physically

- Preview

- Select or Create
  Questions

- Set Study Length

- Place Control ❏'s

GETTING READY TO READ

Both previewing and completing the SELF inventory have influenced me greatly. I used to feel like I was jumping blind off a cliff when I had to read. These two concepts alone have changed my fear into anticipation. I'm no longer scared of college reading and that alone makes all the difference in the world.

—*JEANNA MCAFEE*

One concept I have learned to focus on is to look over the information before I start to read. I am able to ready myself and really see if I am completely ready to stay at a level of reading with intent.

—*KIMBERLY BELL*

By using task awareness, I can preview my material and know how big the task is and what I'm going to do to tackle it.

—*ANGELA JENSEN*

A few minutes of preparation before beginning to read can make as significant difference for you as it has for the college students quoted above. Getting ready to read is the first stage in BICUM study-reading. You will learn to focus your attention and direct your mind to the task of concentrating on textbook material. Taking a few minutes to clear your mind of daily concerns before you read will help you be less distracted when you try to read. Although getting ready takes extra time up front, your reading experience will be so much more effective that you may never again just "jump into" an assignment.

An analogy can be drawn between reading textbooks and playing sports. For example, if you played on a basketball team, you would spend hours learning and practicing such techniques (strategies) as dribbling, shooting, and passing. You would continuously learn about yourself as a player. Recognizing any weak areas, you would consciously work to improve them. Knowing your strengths would enhance your performance during competition. In addition, you would probably want to find information about the teams you would be playing. Having this advance knowledge could give you an edge in the games.

Similarly, you are more likely to find success in reading textbooks if you learn and practice study-reading skills. In reading, as in basketball, effective preparation and regular practice will improve your performance. In this **Ready** stage, you will learn some strategies that will help you discover more about yourself as a reader and about the textbook chapters you will be reading. Recognizing both your weak and strong points and working with them will help you improve your skills in reading. Also, knowing in advance what challenges textbook chapters pose will give you an edge when you face difficulties while reading. Preparation is key to success.

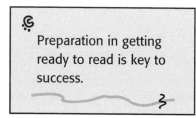

Preparation in getting ready to read is key to success.

SELF Inventory

Each reader is unique, different from any other. No two people read and process information exactly alike. In addition, many factors can influence you each time you sit down to study. For instance, variations in motivation, interests, alertness, and physical well-being all affect comprehension.

Have you ever noticed that sometimes reading a textbook is an easy task, but other times, even if you are trying to read the same textbook, you can barely concentrate on a few words before your mind begins to wander? Obviously, your ability level does not change markedly in a short time period. What then accounts for the contrast in your reading effectiveness?

The answer is probably that sometimes you are simply more ready to read than at other times. Situations change in your life and affect your readiness to concentrate and learn. Times of excitement and happiness can impact your preparedness, just as certainly as times of stress and sadness. Once you recognize and consider some of the possible influences on your reading performance, you can begin to take control and limit their effects.

The word **SELF** is an acronym to remind you of four possible influences on your reading. You will want to inventory each of these crucial factors: **S**tudy Area, **E**motions, **L**evel of Difficulty, and **F**eeling Physically.

S stands for **Study Area**

E stands for **Emotions**

L stands for **Level of Difficulty**

F stands for **Feeling Physically**

The metacognitive information you learn from the SELF inventory will later help you monitor your reading effectiveness. Developing metacognitive skills puts you in charge of your learning. Remember that you are learning to take control of your reading experiences. You are learning to become your own best teacher.

Use the information from your SELF inventory to monitor your reading effectiveness.

S Stands for Study Area

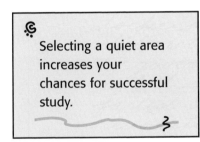

Selecting a quiet area increases your chances for successful study.

Are you studying in a place that is conducive to learning? Quiet areas that are free from distractions are usually the best for reading textbooks. Noise can be a serious deterrent to successful study. Studying in high traffic areas where people are talking and laughing is not a good idea. You will likely be tempted to notice their actions or follow their conversations. Generally, your mind can only concentrate on one message at a time. Conflicting messages can easily pull your attention away from your reading, particularly if you are already bored with the subject. Obviously, it is a waste of time to read a passage over and over again just because noise is interfering with understanding and absorbing the information. Therefore, whenever possible, select a quiet study area because you will have a greater chance for successful study.

For many, the library is a natural place to learn. It is relatively free from distractions, has a quiet atmosphere, and has needed reference books close at hand. One research study (Troth, 1979) reported that students of similar intelligence who studied in the library earned 0.4 grade points higher than those who studied elsewhere.

Likewise, a quiet area in your apartment may be just as suitable for effective study. Experts suggest selecting a specific study place and, if possible, reserving it for study only. Psychologists say that if you do this, you will condition yourself to be ready to learn when you are in that place. Be careful, though, not to allow yourself to nap or daydream in your study area. If you give in, you will negatively condition your mind to wander or want to sleep the next time you sit down to study. Sometimes preparing your mind to study is half the battle of successful studying.

Some students prefer to study on their beds. They say that being comfortable helps them learn better. For most people, though, this is probably not a good idea. It is important to be comfortable, but be cautious about being too comfortable. The softness of the bed may encourage your mind to drift off. After all, sleeping is usually associated with beds, and that is exactly what you will be tempted to do. This is especially true if you are trying to read a textbook that you are not interested in. Also, sitting up instead of lying down is in itself usually more conducive to focused learning.

Interestingly, some students report that studying in a completely quiet area such as a library actually interferes with their concentration. They say that the silence disturbs them. They describe their successful study sessions as times when they listen to the radio or the television. One student expressed his feelings this way:

> "Listening to radio or television helps me better focus on my reading. I simply can't concentrate when I do not hear some noise. Silence, for me, is deafening!"

It is possible that some people actually do learn better with some background sound often referred to as *white noise*. For example, the sound of a fan or soft instrumental music can actually block out other kinds of interference. Listening to the radio or watching television, though, is probably not the best solution to this situation. The messages of the speakers or performers will usually interfere with your concentration. A better choice of background sound would be classical or baroque music. Research has shown that classical music actually enhances people's ability to concentrate and absorb information. Therefore, if you

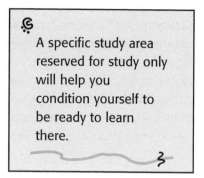

A specific study area reserved for study only will help you condition yourself to be ready to learn there.

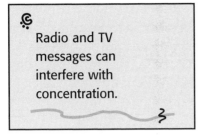

Radio and TV messages can interfere with concentration.

usually listen to the radio or television when you study, try substituting a tape of classical music such as Handel's *Water Music,* for example. Then consciously notice how your mind responds when you study to music without words compared to radio or television. Repeat this experience several times, checking to see if your concentration level, your understanding, and your retention increases. Discover what types of music work best with your thinking.

METACOGNITIVE TRAINING ACTIVITY
Choosing a Study Area
·ᘓ· MTA 2.1 ·ᘓ·

ᘓ DIRECTIONS:

Select three different study areas.

Study for a half hour in each place and keep a separate list of distractors that you notice while studying in each area. (See pp. 9–10 for review of distractions.)

Create four columns on your paper to record your responses to the items below.

1. List the three areas you chose in the column on the left side.

2. Record the number of external distractions you experienced for each study area in column two.

3. Record the number of internal distractions you experienced for each study area in column three.

4. In the fourth column briefly describe ways to overcome some of the external and internal distractors.

5. Which area had the lowest number of *external* distractions?

6. In which area did you have the lowest number of *internal* distractions?

7. To decide which study area is the best for you, consider both the number of distractors and the ease of overcoming them. Record your *choice* of study area.

8. Explain the *reason(s)* for your selection.

9. Self Grade: _____% and brief justification.

Unfortunately, finding an ideal study area is sometimes not possible, and you cannot always wait to study until such a place is available. Evidence suggests that even though studying in a somewhat noisy area is difficult, it can be done. The secret is to focus intensely on the material you are reading so that your mind naturally blocks out distractions. The ability to tune out other distractors and focus on one specific message is known as the **noisy-party phenomenon.** You probably already have this skill well developed, at least in social settings. Recall the last large party you attended. Likely, there were numerous conversations going on simultaneously. Were you successful in ignoring the conversation of others while focusing on the comments made by your friends? Most people do this quite naturally.

You can use this noisy-party phenomenon while trying to read your textbooks in busy areas. For instance, the next time you are riding a bus, try to squeeze in a bit of study time. Again, the secret is to create an interest in the topic and let your mind take over, blocking out distractors.

This book will discuss a number of strategies to help you learn effectively in less than ideal study conditions. For example, later in this chapter you will learn how to preview a textbook chapter and to use Control □'s to aid your concentration. Other strategies, such as reading quietly out loud can aid your concentration and help you study in a distracting environment. In chapter Five, you will also learn about the benefits of using flash cards to study. For many students using flash cards is another answer for learning effectively in less than ideal study conditions.

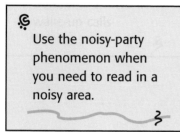

Use the noisy-party phenomenon when you need to read in a noisy area.

E Stands for **Emotions**

Did you know that having an argument with your roommate or breaking up with someone you have been dating can affect your reading comprehension? Intense emotions, either negative or positive, can interfere with your learning. However, since life often has ups and downs, giving up on studying under these circumstances is not a very practical solution.

Actually, you can study while experiencing various emotional levels if you monitor your comprehension

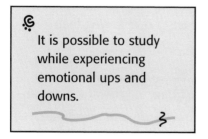

It is possible to study while experiencing emotional ups and downs.

carefully. Consciously taking an inventory of your emotions and being aware that they might interfere with your studies gives you power to moderate the degree of interference from these feelings. Certainly, you should try to improve any situation that you can, but sometimes you might have to study even when your emotions are in an upheaval. When this happens, self-talk such as the following might be helpful:

> "Sure, I'm upset with my roommate. But right now, there is nothing I *can* do to remedy the situation. What I can do is read my economics chapter so I will be prepared for class tomorrow. After I study for about fifty minutes, I will take a walk and decide how I can best solve the problem."

Employing this technique will help you focus on your reading assignment. However, if after a while your mind reverts back to your personal worries, try taking a break and temporarily focus on the concerns. Brainstorming possible options or choices and writing down these ideas might help you identify solutions to your problems and lessen your concerns. Sometimes just recording what is bothering you or talking to someone helps improve the situation. After taking time out to address your personal concerns, recommit to focus on the content of the chapter and continue your reading. By closely monitoring yourself, you can gradually reduce the overall negative effects that emotions can have on your reading effectiveness.

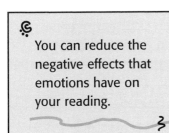

You can reduce the negative effects that emotions have on your reading.

L Stands for **Level of Difficulty**

The difficulty level of a chapter is another factor that can influence your success in reading. If you know in advance that your assignment will be challenging, you can plan to monitor your reading closely. By carefully observing your progress, you are more likely to stay on track and comprehend the material.

What makes material difficult to read? Generally, students find that "boring" information is harder to understand and interesting information is easier to learn. To be sure, having preferences is normal, but be careful not to let your lack of interest in certain subjects get in the way of

> There are no uninteresting subjects. There are only uninterested people.
> —Ralph Nichols

> The more you know about a subject, the easier it is to learn new material.

your learning. Often students lament, "I can't learn _____; it is just not interesting." This mind-set prevents them from learning the material they have labeled negatively. Recognize that your natural areas of interest are changeable, that you can modify and expand what appeals to you. Ralph Nichols once wrote, "There are no uninteresting subjects. There are only uninterested people." You have the ability to change from an uninterested person to an interested person who finds excitement and value in many subjects. In other words, for the most part you can determine which subjects are boring or interesting.

If you consciously decide to expand your areas of interest, you may notice a decline in both the number of boring textbooks and in the number of difficult textbooks. You may even notice an excitement for learning in general. The famous philosopher, John Stuart Mill, referred to such enthusiasm as being characteristic of a "cultivated mind" He described such a person as one who "finds sources of inexhaustible interest in all that surrounds him: the object of nature, the achievements of art, the imagination of poetry, the incidents of history, the ways of mankind, past and present, and their prospects in the future." Can you imagine how much easier and more enjoyable your college years would be if you developed such a mind-set?

Another factor that affects the level of difficulty is lack of background knowledge. E.D. Hirsch discusses the importance of an adequate knowledge base in his book *Cultural Literacy: What Every American Needs to Know*. He makes the important point that the more we know about any given subject the easier it is to learn additional information on that subject. For example, if a biology major and a beginning biology student were to read from the same course text, the advanced student would probably learn the information more easily and retain it much longer than the novice student. One reason for the difference is that the experienced student already has a well developed **mental schema,** or background knowledge, in biology, which serves as a foundation on which to build. (The importance of using mental schema is explained on page 41.)

The challenge of developing adequate background knowledge in many subject areas can sometimes seem overwhelming. According to Pulitzer Prize winner Ronald Kotulak, author of *Inside the Brain*, the human brain continues to grow and build information throughout a person's life. As a college student you are continually being exposed to new ideas in a variety of subject areas. Therefore you are in an excellent position to develop your schema rapidly. Your age and mental maturity will give you a decided advantage over young children. Your life's experiences have already helped you build a scaffolding or skeleton of knowledge to which you can add as you read and learn. Since reading is such an important tool in developing schema, the more you read, the faster your schema will develop.

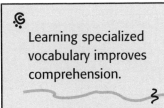

You can build your background knowledge if you are weak in a subject.

If you find that you do not have sufficient background information in one of your classes, try to locate another textbook that is written for a less advanced audience. Also, reading a general overview of the information from the encyclopedia might be helpful. You might consider meeting with your instructor for additional guidance in how to gain the missing information. Tutors are another source of assistance because they are often trained specifically in how to help students who have gaps in background knowledge.

New college students are often surprised at the number of difficult, unfamiliar vocabulary words they find in their college textbooks. Consequently, they may feel overwhelmed with the reading, not recognizing that learning the new words is a vehicle to acquire the specialized language necessary to operate in any field of study. According to Brenda D. Smith, author of numerous college reading texts, students need to learn approximately 20,000 new vocabulary words during their college career. She states that as students study to become experts in their chosen field of interest, they will need to learn its specialized vocabulary. Smith gives encouragement by observing that once students overcome the initial difficulty of learning unknown terminology, comprehension improves and the reading becomes easier (Smith 1987).

Learning specialized vocabulary improves comprehension.

Sometimes people have the mistaken idea that the best way to learn new words is to memorize them in lists. However, this technique usually is not effective because thinking is not done in isolated words; instead language is acquired through meaningful thought units, or *chunks*. A much more effective approach to learning vocabulary is to figure out the meaning of words through the use of contextual clues. Understanding the precise meaning of each word is usually not necessary as long as you get the essence of how each word contributes to what the speaker or writer is trying to communicate. For most students, stopping to define unfamiliar words interrupts the message or conversation, and they usually must reread some material in order to reconnect with the author's train of thought.

Recognize that gaining a better vocabulary is an ongoing and natural process. Language is initially developed by hearing others speak. According to Dr. C. Ray Graham, a linguistics professor from Brigham Young University, children have a natural ability to acquire language. From around age two to eight years they gain about twelve to fifteen new vocabulary words every day. Our preliminary understanding of the word may be somewhat vague, but as we continue to hear it, our understanding becomes more refined.

For example, our first association with the word *dog* may lead us to believe that any furry creature is a dog. Our inexact definition may include rabbits, cats, and other small animals. But as we continue to hear the word *dog* used in other contexts we eliminate other furry creatures from our definition. This natural process that we have used since childhood to build and refine our vocabulary through listening and speaking also occurs in adult reading. Granted, the words are more complex in college textbook reading, but essentially the process is the same.

Authors want to assist you in the process of vocabulary acquisition. One of the ways that they do this is to first emphasize the important words by bolding or italicizing them, followed by a clear definition of how the words are used in context. Notice how the concept of "personal space" is introduced and defined in the following example:

> The buffer zone that we like to maintain around our bodies is known as **personal space.** Its size may vary according to culture, family habits, and how well we know the person standing near us.

Table 2.1 illustrates common clues that authors use to define new terms.

Using contextual clues is perhaps one of the best ways to learn new words, although there are other useful methods for vocabulary acquisition. It is helpful to remember that in attacking new words there is a suggested order. One very successful student, Kathy Convey, suggested the acronym **CPA** as a memory device for ways to learn new words:

TABLE 2.1   CLUES TO WORDS BEING DEFINED IN CONTEXT

Clues	Examples
Using clue words such as *is*, *means*, and *is defined as*.	Aggression *is* physical or verbal behavior intended to hurt someone. When someone feels that they are competent and effective this *means* they have high self-efficacy.
Using contrast with another term.	Some individuals seem to have an innate sense of security and trust in their own decisions and actions. *In contrast*, individuals who use social comparison evaluate their opinions and abilities by comparing themselves to others. A cult is characterized by (1) the distinctive ritual of its devotion to a god or a person, (2) isolation from the surrounding "evil" culture, and (3) a charismatic leader. A sect, *by contrast* is a spinoff from a major religion.
Using punctuation signals such as commas, dashes, semicolons, and parentheses.	Oftentimes when students are diagnosed with a learning disability, they also experience learned helplessness, feeling little control over the events of their lives. Many small communities experience **cohesiveness**—a feeling of being bound together by a common cause.

C = Contextual clues (surrounding text)

P = Parts of the word (prefixes, roots, suffixes)

A = Authoritative source (instructor, dictionary)

This acronym will be explained in the paragraphs that follow. Try using it to help you remember the order for figuring out unfamiliar terms.

The **C** in CPA stands for using *context,* which means reading without stopping to look up words. This is the least distracting method for gaining meaning because it does not interfere with the flow of reading. According to Jenkins, et al. (1989), using context clues can be useful, although sometimes misleading. Nevertheless, there is ample evidence that instruction in using context clues is effective for learning new words. Although this method is not an exact science, in most cases it will save time and allow you to make intelligent guesses about the definition of new words.

Additional clues to the meaning of unfamiliar vocabulary can be found through *word parts*, which is what the **P** represents in CPA. Since many word parts in English and other languages have Greek or Latin origins, learning the meanings of these parts can help unlock the definition of many unknown words. For example, according to Glazier (1993), if you know that the word part *syn-* means *together* or *with,* you have a clue to the meaning of more than 450 other words.

The **A** in the CPA acronym helps you to remember that when necessary you should consult an *authoritative source.* This should be any credible source, such as course instructors, tutors, glossaries, or dictionaries. Referring to one of these sources can often clear up comprehension blocks and open the door to increased understanding. It is probably best to utilize authoritative resources only when comprehension breaks down, because consulting them can be time-consuming and can interfere with comprehension.

F Stands for Feeling Physically

How you feel physically affects your success in reading textbooks. Simply stated, good health enhances the ability to learn, but discomfort such as pain or fatigue interferes. Even minor physical discomforts can disrupt effective study. Attend to pressing physical needs before you attempt to read textbooks—it can improve your concentration later. Answer the questions in the survey in Table 2.2 to identify specific needs that you might take care of before beginning to study. Although these physical distractors may seem obvious, some students discount their influence and consequently allow them to impact negatively their study time.

Even though physical distractors are common, it is easy to overlook their influence on your concentration. Consciously reminding yourself to attend to them can improve your overall study effectiveness. For example, if you are sleepy, try pausing for a short power nap. Find a quiet, preferably dimly lit place with a bed or comfortable chair,

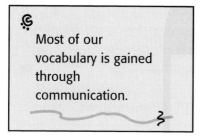

Most of our vocabulary is gained through communication.

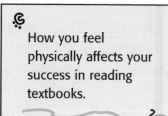

How you feel physically affects your success in reading textbooks.

TABLE 2.2   PHYSICAL DISTRACTOR SURVEY

Questions	If answer is	Correct by
1. Am I sleepy?	Yes	Take a power nap.
2. Am I hungry?	Yes	Eat a healthy snack.
3. Am I thirsty?	Yes	Drink a glass of water.
4. Am I too hot or cold?	Yes	Adjust the thermostat. Put on or take off a piece of clothing.
5. Are my clothes comfortable?	No	Change into sweats or other loose-fitting clothes.
6. Do I feel sluggish?	Yes	Take a brisk walk.

and doze off for a few minutes. Be sure to set an alarm or alert someone to call you when your time is up. Generally, you should limit your naps to no more than thirty minutes because napping too long can actually increase your sense of fatigue. Also, lengthy naps can interrupt your sleep cycle and prevent you from sleeping at your normal bedtime. Distractors in the other areas of the survey (i.e., hunger, thirst, body temperature, clothing comfort, and general alertness) might also be readily adjusted to enhance your learning.

Everyday Physical Care

Short-term attention to bodily needs is helpful, but even more important to your mental alertness is the everyday care you give to your body. Realize that there are definite connections between what you eat, how you feel physically, and how you perform mentally. Take time to eat a balanced diet. Refer to the Food Guide Pyramid (Figure 2.1) for a reminder of the six food groups and the suggested daily servings for each.

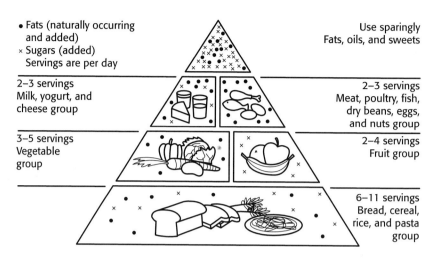

U.S. Department of Agriculture Food Guide Pyramid.

FIGURE 2.1 FOOD GUIDE PYRAMID

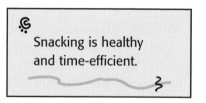

Snacking is healthy and time-efficient.

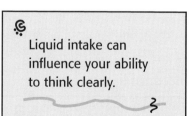

Liquid intake can influence your ability to think clearly.

In past years nutritionists advised eating three main meals a day with no snacking in between. However, recent research indicates that eating five or six mini-meals throughout the day is actually more beneficial to the body. Not only is snacking a healthy alternative to large meals, but it is also more time-efficient for those with busy schedules.

If you decide to be a snacker, be sure to include nutritious foods in your assortment of snacks. Fresh fruits and vegetables are naturally healthy and require little preparation. Be cautious of eating too many processed fat-free products, as these foods still contain calories, especially from sugar. Also, since many fat-free products have very little fiber, you may be tempted to overeat in order to feel satisfied. You're better off eating natural foods with more fiber, even if you consume a few fat grams in the process.

In addition, regularly drinking enough liquid is important as you prepare physically to succeed with your study-reading. Water is a major part of your physical makeup. In fact, sixty percent of the total human mass is water. You have probably heard that you should drink six to eight glasses of water a day. You may be like many people who find this guide difficult to follow. However, if you remember to drink a tall (16 oz.) glass of water when you first arise in the morning, sip a 16-oz. water bottle during the day, and then drink another tall (16 oz.) glass once you arrive home at night, you will have consumed six of the eight recommended glasses. If you find time to drink the other two glasses of water some other time during the day, that is fine. If not, just remember to make a conscious effort to increase your liquid intake.

Fruit juices are good substitutes for some of the recommended water. However, drinking carbonated beverages instead of water is not nearly so beneficial. Recognize that if you do not drink an adequate supply of liquid, your brain may not be able to function at its peak performance. If you are serious about concentrating as you read, drink a glass of water before beginning your study session—it will actually help increase needed oxygen in the brain.

The amount and quality of your sleep will also influence your ability to think clearly. Studies indicate that the number of sleep hours needed varies considerably among students. Some students require only five or six hours of sleep a night, while others need as many as nine or ten. For most students, six to eight hours of sleep is adequate. However, some students sleep a sufficient number of hours but still feel tired. In order to be restful, sleep should be long, deep, and continuous. By going to bed and arising at regular times, you will program your internal biological clock so that you will "sleep when you are sleeping and be awake when you are awake." You will probably feel more alert during your study time if you are adequately rested.

A discussion about the connection between how you feel physically and how successfully you read would not be complete without including a few comments about regular exercise. Since everyone can benefit from regular exercise, if you do not already have a program, consider participating in an aerobic activity at least three times a week. Exercising for sustained twenty-minute intervals will improve your overall conditioning. As a result, you will feel healthier, and your reading and thinking will improve. Remember to consult your doctor before beginning a strenuous exercise program.

Going to bed and getting up at regular times programs your internal biological clock.

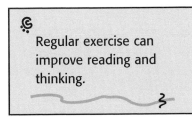

Regular exercise can improve reading and thinking.

SELF Inventory Results

Try to clear up any weak areas you noticed in your SELF inventory before you begin study-reading. If possible, select a more favorable study area, work through your

Monitor your reading more closely if you have physical distractors that you cannot change.

emotional distractors, prepare for difficult reading, and get yourself physically ready to read. However, in situations where you currently can do nothing to improve your circumstances, do not decide to give up. Plan instead to monitor your reading closely. Recognize that knowing in advance that these SELF factors may compete for your attention while you are reading gives you the power to weaken their influence. Your conscious choices can reduce their negative effects in these crucial areas.

Preview Your Reading

One of the most important techniques that is often forgotten by students is **previewing.** It involves conducting a brief overview of the contents of the chapter before reading. Quickly leafing through the pages will provide you with a "big picture" of the chapter organization. After viewing the chapter as a whole, the details will make more sense when you begin reading. Creating a mental framework will provide a way to organize the information to be learned. This strategy does not require much time. Usually *five minutes* of previewing is sufficient for an assignment that will take about an hour to read. Students who begin to use this strategy report significant positive results from the few minutes invested in previewing.

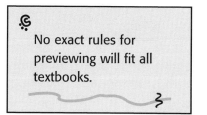

No exact rules for previewing will fit all textbooks.

There are several parts of the chapter to notice in your preview. However, since there are many different writing styles and printing formats, no exact set of rules for previewing will fit all textbooks. Nevertheless, the following parts are frequently included in textbook chapters and will contain valuable information.

Notice the Title

Titles are created to attract attention and to limit or identify specific subjects covered in the chapters. Use the title as a starting place to begin focusing your thoughts. If you are like most college students, you have many responsibilities each day and are involved in numerous

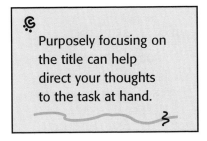

Purposely focusing on the title can help direct your thoughts to the task at hand.

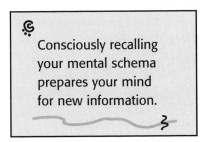

It is easier to learn information that you already know something about.

Consciously recalling your mental schema prepares your mind for new information.

activities. Besides schoolwork, obligations associated with family, friends, work, church, etc. fill your mind. As a result, concentrating on a reading assignment can seem next to impossible. Fortunately, by purposely focusing on the title of a chapter, you can begin to direct your thoughts to the task at hand. As you read the title, ask yourself the following question:

"What do I already know about this subject?"

Any material that you can recall that is related to the chapter will make learning the new information easier. Since your mind stores information in *thought units*, previous knowledge can serve as hooks on which to hang new related information. As mentioned earlier, it is easier to learn information that you already know something about.

This mental schema helps prepare your mind for additional material. The majority of educational researchers, including Anderson (1994) believe that a reader's schema is critical to comprehending, learning, and remembering material. Consciously recalling what you already know about the subject improves overall retention of new material. For example, if a chapter title in your history textbook is "The Jury System," you might recall some comments by someone who has served on a jury. Or, most people can easily remember some information about juries from television shows or trials of famous people. Recalling any background information you have about juries could be helpful. By consciously retrieving data that is stored in your memory, you will increase your ability to learn new information. Purposely connecting the information that you already know to new material that you want to learn is a powerful memory technique.

Read the Introduction and the Summary

Next, read the introduction and/or summary to the chapter. Textbooks often print information three times. In the introduction, the author describes what he or she is going to tell you. In the body of the chapter, he or she describes the information in detail. In the summary, the author reviews the contents of the chapter. It has been demonstrated that if you read the two condensed versions before reading the detailed explanation or body of the chapter, you will better understand and remember the information. Many college students report significant improvement when they have advance knowledge of textbook material. Identifying ahead of time what the chapter is about helps your mind more effectively organize the information in the chapter. This is another effective memory technique called **advance organizing.** Organized information is much easier to understand and remember.

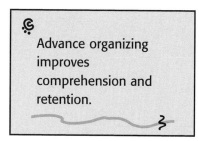

Advance organizing improves comprehension and retention.

Check the Headings and Subheadings

Now, flip through the entire chapter, reading the headings and subheadings. Together these are actually an outline of the topics, main ideas, and supporting details. Notice the size of the print and the placement on the page. Authors often identify main headings by using darker and larger type. Also, the headings that are centered or aligned with the left margin often lead to the main points, and the subheadings indented like a paragraph frequently indicate supporting details. Focusing on these headings is an essential step in getting the "big picture" or creating a mental framework of the chapter. However, if your textbook only has a limited number of headings and subheadings, such as those used in philosophy, you can still get an partial overview of the chapter by reading the first sentence in each paragraph.

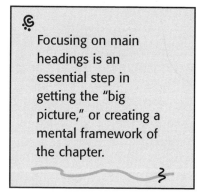

Focusing on main headings is an essential step in getting the "big picture," or creating a mental framework of the chapter.

Some experts recommend also reading the first paragraph under each of the headings and subheadings and the first sentence in each paragraph. This technique is sometimes referred to as *skimming* and may give the gist or essence of the chapter being previewed. Because including these strategies takes extra time, you might want to use them regularly only after you have determined their value to you. Try reading these parts in each of your textbooks to decide if the amount of information you obtain is worth the time you spend.

Check the Bold and Italicized Print

Notice any additional **bold** or *italicized* print throughout the chapter. These words are important terms or key concepts that the author wants you to be sure to notice. You can often learn the meaning of these words by reading the surrounding information. Recall the earlier discussion on context and using CPA.

If you are unable to figure out the meaning of bold or italicized words from the context, check to see if they are defined in a glossary at the end of the book. You may decide to look up the definitions of unfamiliar words before reading the chapter, which is certainly an option. Certainly, knowing their meanings in advance would make your reading experience easier. However, looking up a list of words can be time-consuming. Try doing this in a couple of your study sessions and notice if doing so makes a big difference in your reading effectiveness. If it does, then pause for a few moments in your preview and figure out the definitions of these words. If defining terms prior to reading is not that helpful, then continue with your preview, but make a note to learn the meanings of these words later. Bolded or italicized words have a high probability of showing up on quizzes and examinations, especially in introductory, general education courses.

Utilize the Charts, Maps, Graphs, and Diagrams

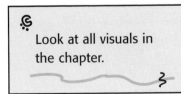

Look at all visuals in the chapter.

Be sure to look at all visuals in the chapter. They can be a tremendous benefit in improving comprehension. The old cliché "a picture is worth a thousand words" definitely applies to reading textbook graphics. Authors know that visuals can clarify points, show relationships, and depict information that is confusing when text alone is used.

Inspect the visuals, reading the labels and identifying key information. Ask yourself: "What is the purpose of each visual and what is the message being conveyed?" Be sure to notice the trends in the data and locate the extremes in

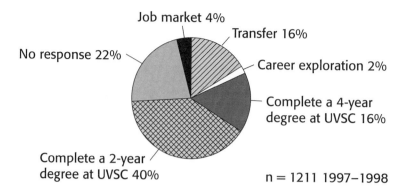

PRIMARY REASON FOR ATTENDING COLLEGE AT UVSC

Source: Utah Valley State College, Office of Institutional Research and Strategic Planning

FIGURE 2.2 READING A PIE CHART

charts and graphs. Usually the high and low points contain the information you will need to remember for testing purposes. Later as you read the chapter, refer again to the visuals and notice their connection to the text. You may then further refine your interpretation of the messages each visual presents.

For example, look at the **pie chart** in Figure 2.2. What do you learn about the reasons students attend Utah Valley State College (UVSC), the authors' school?

The two primary reasons students attend UVSC are practical ones such as to *complete a degree* and *transfer to other colleges*. The least mentioned reason for attending UVSC is for *career exploration*. At the bottom of the figure, the source of the information is written in small print. Also included are the number of students surveyed ($n = 1211$) and the date the survey was given (1997–1998). Both of these pieces of information are important to know. Large numbers are usually more representative of the total population than are small numbers, and new data is usually more relevant and useful than older information.

What information does the **bar graph** in Figure 2.3 portray? This figure depicts the mean age of students attending UVSC. The information is divided into years according to when the survey was taken. Note how significantly the student body has changed in the five years. It would be interesting to know why the mean age of the students has decreased by two years in a relatively short

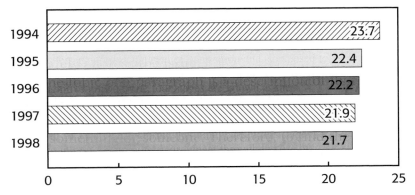

Source: Utah Valley State College, Office of Institutional Research and Management Studies

FIGURE 2.3 READING A BAR GRAPH

time period. The source of this information is the Office of Institutional Research and Management Studies at Utah Valley State College.

Make Predictions

Now that you have looked over the chapter, you should have a good idea of what material will be covered. Combine this information with your background knowledge of the subject and predict what you think the author has written. Anticipate how the major points will be explained and what information will be used as supporting details.

For example, if you preview a chapter entitled "Defense Mechanisms" in your psychology book you might try to think of some of your own defense mechanisms and predict how a discussion on them might develop. For example, if you think of one of the most common defense mechanisms, rationalization (making excuses for your behavior), try to recall some instances when you tried to justify your behavior. Thinking about situations that are familiar to you will not only help you anticipate the upcoming text discussion but might also help you make meaningful associations that can in turn increase your interest level while reading.

By including predictions in your preview, you are more likely to stay focused when you read.

By including predictions in your preview, you are more likely to stay focused when you read. Later, as you move through the chapter, you can verify your predictions and make adjustments when your thoughts do not match what is written. Some students find it useful to write their predictions. They say it is easier to check them and compare the written copy with the text.

To improve your skill in accurately predicting what information will be tested on exams, it is important to practice this technique. One way to do that is to verify your predictions as you read.

Create an Interest

The entire learning process becomes easier when you are interested in the topic. Make a conscious effort to watch for appealing facts or useful ideas. If you do not find a topic naturally inviting, try asking those who like the subject what they find interesting about it. Also, consciously looking for possible useful information can help motivate you to find purpose in what you are reading. Usually the more inviting you find a reading assignment, the more easily it can be understood and retained.

You might consider making it a personal challenge to find something interesting and worthwhile in every one of your reading assignments. While you are previewing, if you decide that reading a chapter will be a productive experience, that usually will be the case. You can direct your mind to learn by telling yourself that the material you are reading is interesting. Once you decide that a chapter is valuable, you can consciously create an interest in the material. Remember, you are the one in control, not the textbook

For instance, if you preview a history text selection on Supreme Court Justices, you might find it interesting to learn that Sandra Day O'Connor was the first woman Supreme Court Justice. This could lead to consideration of what characteristics she possessed that helped her overcome gender bias and reach this high office. As your interest increases, reading about her and other justices would be more enjoyable.

METACOGNITIVE TRAINING ACTIVITY
Previewing
·୧· MTA 2.2 ·୧·

⅜ DIRECTIONS:

Please number your responses and put the title and number of the MTA at the top of your report.

Preview one of your textbook chapters and respond to the following items.

1. Record the title of the course, text, and chapter.

2. List three aids contained in the chapter that helped you to preview.

3. Do you have any previous knowledge that will assist you in understanding what is contained in the chapter? Explain.

4. Glance at the visuals. What kinds of information are they displaying?

5. What parts of the chapter will be of most interest to you? Explain.

6. Write a prediction about what might be discussed in this chapter.

After reading the chapter, evaluate the effectiveness of using previewing.

7. Was your prediction correct? Why or why not?

8. Was previewing beneficial in helping you with the actual reading of the chapter? Why or why not?

9. Do you think that you will use previewing in the future? Explain.

10. Self Grade: _____% and brief justification.

Select or Create Questions

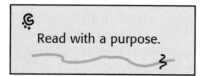

Read with a purpose.

Successful readers are students who **read with a purpose.** They read to answer questions. You may have noticed when you previewed your textbook chapter that there were questions already created for you (often located at either the beginning or end of the chapter). The answers to these questions are usually what the author considers to be the most important material in the chapter and often are found on quizzes and exams. Looking over these questions before you read the chapter makes finding the answers a lot easier. Many students report that after looking over questions, the answers seem to stand out when they read their textbook chapters. This practice is much more efficient than randomly searching for answers after reading information. You will save time if you make this strategy part of your study plan.

If your textbook does not include questions, you can create your own questions. Simply place question words (Who, What, Why, When, Where, or How) in front of the headings or subheadings. Look at the following example.

Heading: "Ecosystems,"

Questions: "What are ecosystems?" or

             "How do ecosystems work?"

Forming questions and searching for answers helps you to stay involved and direct your own reading. The result is that you are more likely to stay on track.

Set Study Length

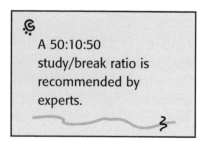

A 50:10:50 study/break ratio is recommended by experts.

Setting study length includes both determining the length of time you plan to study and selecting the number of pages you plan to read in that amount of time. Experts often recommend that readers study for 50 minutes, take a 10-minute break, then study for another 50 minutes. This study/break ratio of 50:10:50 suggests that you will likely be able to concentrate for just under an hour before your mind begins to wander. The 10-minute break will refresh you and

---

METACOGNITIVE TRAINING ACTIVITY
Selecting or Creating Questions
·ᔔ· MTA 2.3 ·ᔔ·

ᔔ DIRECTIONS:

Record the MTA number and title at the top of your paper.

Fold your paper lengthwise. As you select or create questions, write them on the left side of your paper. Then later put your answers on the right side.

From a textbook select a chapter that you need to master for an exam.

Follow the directions below, and respond carefully to each item.

Label and/or number your responses.

---

1. Are there questions included in the chapter? If so, record at least five of the questions. If the chapter does not have questions, create five of your own by turning the headings into questions.

NOTE: Read the chapter and consciously search for answers to the questions.

2. Write the answers to your five questions on the right side of your paper.

3. In your opinion will these questions likely appear on an exam? Why or why not?

4. Self Grade _____% and brief justification.

> ᔔ
> Concentration is a skill that you can develop with practice.

---

allow time for your mind to absorb and consolidate the information you have worked with for the past 50 minutes. Research studies indicate that students actually learn more by taking 10-minute breaks than when they study for several hours without stopping.

If you cannot stay focused for 50 minutes, try an alternate study/break ratio such as 30:10:30 or 15:10:15. Each time you study set a time limit and notice if your mind stays focused for that duration. The key is to stretch your attentions span slightly past your present capabilities. Concentration is a skill that you can develop with practice.

Remember, you can be in control of your learning. Once you find a study length that matches your current capabilities, study for that length of time; then take a break. Gradually expand your study sessions to reach the recommended 50-minute time block. Starting out with short study sessions and working your way up to the 50 minute time is much preferred to unfocused longer study sessions. You will find that setting a beginning and end to your studying will help you concentrate better. It is motivating to know you have a 10-minute break when you complete your study session.

After you have set the length of your study session, you should then determine how many pages you think you will be able to cover. Many students have little or no idea of how much time it takes them to read textbooks. On one occasion, students were asked to predict their reading time for a three-page assignment. Their estimates ranged from five minutes to three hours. In actuality, most of the students finished in twenty minutes.

If you are like these students and really do not know how fast you read, just make a rough estimate. Then when you actually read the assignment, notice how many pages you cover in a specific time. If you notice your reading speed on several occasions, you will soon be able to predict quite accurately how many pages you can cover in a specific time. Once you know how fast you read, begin to extend the number of pages you plan to cover in a study session. Did you know that you can actually read faster simply by pushing yourself? For example, if you usually read ten pages in 50 minutes, try to read eleven pages the next time you study. Most students find that they can read the additional page quite easily within the allotted time. Choosing a specific number of pages to read improves your focus on the material and helps you more effectively pace yourself as your read.

Place Control □ 's

By using the first four strategies listed in the Ready stage, you have accumulated a great deal of information about both the textbook chapter you are preparing to read

METACOGNITIVE TRAINING ACTIVITY
Study Sessions
·ʓ· MTA 2.4 ·ʓ·

ʓ DIRECTIONS:

Try to study for at least 50 minutes before taking a 10-minute study break.

1. Record both the time you begin and the time that you end your study. Predict how many pages you will be able to cover.

2. Record the number of minutes you were able to stay focused without being distracted and the number of pages read.

3. Were you able to study effectively for the suggested 50 minutes before you took a break? Why or why not?

4. What could you do to increase your effectiveness in the following categories?
   a. staying focused for 50 minutes
   b. only taking a ten minute study break
   c. getting back on task after the break

5. How did these sessions compare, in terms of accomplishment, to your previous study sessions?

6. Self Grade: _____% and brief justification.

Continue to plan and monitor your study times, extending your sessions by 5-minute increments until you reach the 50:10:50 study/break ratio.

> Metacognition will help you gain control over your reading.

and about yourself as a reader. Now you are ready to use this knowledge to set up a self-awareness monitoring system that will help keep you focused as you read. Increasing awareness of your mental processing (metacognition) will help you gain control over your reading.

You can prevent the problem of allowing material you do not understand to pass by your mind unnoticed by using a powerful monitoring technique called **Placing Control □'s.** To use this strategy, carefully select logical stopping places in your textbook chapter before you begin to read. Next, draw a small box at each of these points. Then as you read, these boxes will serve as signals to stop and check your comprehension. As you pause to process the information, you have several options. For example, you can simply ask yourself if you fully understand what you just read. An even better choice you can use in assessing your knowledge is to try to *paraphrase* the information or put it into your own words. By doing this, you begin to internalize the information you are studying, which then enhances memorization. Once you have analyzed your comprehension level, you can then place a check (✓) in the Control Box to indicate your understanding. Continue to read to the next box and repeat this process. (See the section in chapter 6 on Personalizing BICUM for other ways to mark the Control Boxes that show more levels of discrimination in understanding.)

Before drawing the Control □'s, there are several points you should consider. Begin by using the information you gained about your reading readiness from the SELF inventory to help you decide how many boxes you will need to place. For example, if you have a lot of internal worries, a poor study area, or very difficult material, you will need to monitor your reading more closely.

Remember to place your Control □'s after your preview, but *before* actually beginning to read the chapter. You will need to visibly mark these stopping places with a pencil or pen as shown in Figure 2.4. It is best to place the control boxes in natural stopping places, which are often signaled by the author's organizational structure such as headings and subheadings. Because you place these boxes yourself, and because they stand out from the printed text, they should catch your attention while you read.

Later, as you read you will stop at the control boxes you have placed and test your understanding by simply asking yourself what you have just read. If you understand the material you should be able to put the information into your own words. If you are unable to paraphrase the author's message, you probably do not understand it well enough to continue reading. In chapter 3, you will be given suggestions, called fix-up strategies to help you correct comprehension problems.

Control □'s can help you stay focused while reading. Have you ever have had the experience of reading a

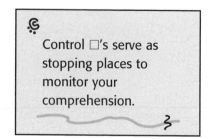

Paraphrasing what you read helps you assess your level of comprehension.

Control □'s serve as stopping places to monitor your comprehension.

The Nature of Ecosystems

Overview of the Participants

Diverse natural systems abound on the Earth's surface. In climate, landforms, soil, vegetation, animal life, and other features, deserts differ from hardwood forests, which differ from tundra and prairies. In biodiversity and physical properties, seas differ from reefs, which differ from lakes. *Yet despite the differences, such systems are alike in many aspects of their structure and function.*

With few exceptions, each system runs on energy that plants and other photosynthesizers capture from the sun. Photosynthesizers, recall, are the most common autotrophs (self-feeders). They convert sunlight energy to chemical energy, which they use to construct organic compounds from inorganic raw materials. By securing energy from the environment, autotrophs are **primary producers** for the entire system.

All other organisms in the system are heterotrophs, not self-feeders. They extract energy from compounds that primary producers put together. **Consumers** feed on the tissues of other organisms. The consumers called *herbivores* eat plants, *carnivores* eat animals, *omnivores* eat both, and *parasites* extract energy from living hosts that they live in or on. Still other heterotrophs, called **decomposers,** include fungi and bacteria that obtain energy by breaking down the remains or products of organisms. Other, the **detritivores,** obtain nutrients from decomposing particles of organic matter. Crabs and earthworms are example of detritivores.

Autotrophs secure nutrients as well as energy for the entire system. During growth, they take up water and carbon dioxide (as sources of oxygen, carbon, and hydrogen) and dissolved minerals (including nitrogen and phosphorus). Such materials are building blocks for carbohydrates, lipids, proteins, and nucleic acids. When decomposers and detritivores consume organic matter, they break it down to small inorganic molecules. Unless something removes the molecules from the system, as by runoff from a meadow, the autotrophs can use the molecules again as nutrients.

What we have just described in broad outline is an ecosystem. An **ecosystem** is an array of organisms and their physical environment, all interacting through a one-way flow of energy and a cycling of materials. It is an open system, unable to sustain itself. Each ecosystem requires an *energy input* (as from the sun) and often *nutrient inputs* (as from a creek that delivers dissolved minerals to a lake). It has energy and nutrient outputs. Energy cannot be recycled; in time, most of the energy that autotrophs fixed is lost to the environment, mainly as metabolic heat. Nutrients do get cycled, but some are still lost. Most of this chapter deals with the inputs, internal transfers, and outputs of ecosystems. ☐

Structure of Ecosystems

Trophic Levels   The organisms of an ecosystem can be classified in terms of their functions in a hierarchy of feeding relationships, call trophic levels (from *troph,* meaning nourishment). ""Who eats whom?'' we an ask. As organism B eats organism A, energy gets transferred to B from A. All organisms at a given trophic level are the same number of transfer steps away from an energy input into the ecosystem. . . . Being closest to the energy input into this system (sunlight), trees and other primary producers are the *first trophic level.* Primary consumers—which feed directly on primary producers—include herbivores (such as leaf-eating larvae of moths) and detritivores (such as earthworms that feed on fallen leaves). Primary consumers are at the *second trophic level.* At the *third level,* we find primary carnivores (a variety of beetles, spiders, and birds) that prey on primary consumers. At the *fourth level* are secondary carnivores, such as owls, that feed on species of the third trophic level.

By this classification, then, all organisms at a given trophic level have the same sets of predators, prey, or both. But remember this qualification: many decomposers, people, and other omnivores feed at several trophic levels, so they must be partitioned among levels or assigned to one of their own.

Food Webs   Often a straight-line sequence of who eats whom in an ecosystem is called a **food chain.** You will have a hard time finding such simple, isolated cases. Why? Most often, the same food source is a part of more than one chain, especially when it is at low trophic levels. It is much more accurate to think of food chains as *cross-connecting* with one another—that is, as **food webs.** ☐

FIGURE 2.4 SAMPLE OF PLACING CONTROL BOXES (☐'s)

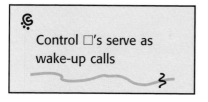

Control □'s serve as wake-up calls

paragraph or an entire page without any idea what was said. This occurs for several reasons. You may be thinking of personal concerns, things to be done or even unconsciously avoiding the task at hand. When you see these Control □'s and stop to check your understanding, allow them to also serve as *wake-up calls* to check your concentration. If your mind has wandered, become aware of where your thoughts have strayed. After all, just reading with your eyes is not reading, your mind must be focused on the material.

By stopping periodically, you automatically break up the reading into smaller parts. One advantage of doing this is that the task becomes more manageable. Instead of reading long pages of material, you can determine how much you can handle at a time. Stopping at each box can actually rest your mind by changing the nature of the activity from reading to paraphrasing.

Students who have used Control □'s say they appreciate knowing early on when their understanding begins to falter. Then they only have to return to the previous check mark, instead of rereading large sections. When material is processed in manageable chunks, it is easier to understand and remember. Clearly understood ideas form a strong foundation or schema for learning additional information.

One busy single mother who had many interruptions while reading her text reported that the control boxes helped her to complete her homework despite disturbances. She reported that when returning to her homework after being interrupted, she could instantly tell where she had left off by finding the last unchecked box.

When you are first learning BICUM, you will likely need to place Control □'s more closely together than you will once you know the program. Remember, you are training your mind, and it takes time to do this, as it does with any skill you wish to learn. If you use Control □'s regularly with your reading assignments, you will likely find that your mind will begin to work with you. Most students notice that as they continue to use BICUM, they need fewer and fewer □'s because they are successfully training their mind to stay on task. However, even skilled BICUM readers have times when their readiness to read is low. When many factors are working against them, they should increase the number of Control □'s and place them closely together.

Using this metacognitive system to monitor your comprehension is a step toward becoming an expert reader.

You will begin to recognize times when you understand text material and times when you do not. What at first will take a deliberate effort, with practice will likely become automatic as you seek for meaning while reading.

Is Study-Reading for You?

Does this study-reading system seem a bit overwhelming? Some students feel that way when they see how much work is involved in effective study. They exclaim, "I've spent all this time just getting ready to read, and I haven't even started my assignment yet" or "I don't have time to do all these extra things. I just want to read the chapter and get it over with." If these thoughts are similar to yours, pause for a moment and ask yourself: "Why am I reading this assignment?" If your answer is "I just want to get the assignment finished," then you are right; study-reading is too much work. A quick glance over the material is probably sufficient. However, if this is all you do, recognize that you really are not reading the assignment. In actuality, *reading is reading only when meaning is coming through.* Without comprehension, you really are not reading. You may be looking at words or even voicing them, but unless you understand, you are *not* reading. At best, you are only finishing an assignment, which will do little good in the long run. When exam time arrives, you may not be prepared.

If, however, your answer is "I want to understand and remember the material in the chapter," then study-reading is worth your time. If you are serious about your college studies, then following these study-readings and strategies will help you be successful, and will actually take less time in the long run.

Study-reading does take more time up front, but with practice you will save a great deal of time and will dramatically increase your retention of material. Reading is a skill, and like any other skill, it takes time to develop and improve. As you practice BICUM, you will become more efficient, and you will take less time to complete your assignments. Be assured that if you faithfully "hang in

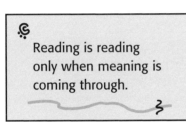

Reading is reading only when meaning is coming through.

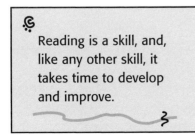

Reading is a skill, and, like any other skill, it takes time to develop and improve.

there," you will join the thousands of other successful readers who readily agree that BICUM training is worth every bit of the time they spend. One busy student reported that time is her most precious commodity. By using the methods explained in this text, she has cut her study time in half. She earns mostly A's in her college courses and believes that being able to comprehend and remember what she reads will positively influence her entire life.

Summary

For many students, reading college textbooks is a frustrating experience. They read page after page of words with little or no comprehension of meaning. However, by following the strategies in the *Ready* stage, you can avoid these experiences and prepare to read efficiently. There are five strategies listed in this stage; you should practice all of them.

The first Ready strategy is the metacognitive SELF inventory, which directs you to modify, eliminate, or prepare for factors that could divert your concentration. Since learning is difficult if you have a lot of distractions, either internally or externally prepare yourself for success by doing the following: You learn to select an appropriate study area, work through emotional distractors, assess the level of difficulty of the material you will be reading, and measure how physically ready you are to study.

The second Ready strategy is previewing. Look over the chapter to get an idea of its contents. Doing this will activate your prior knowledge, help you see the "big picture," and help you find parts in the chapter which are of particular interest to you.

The third Ready preparation technique is selecting questions to help you focus as you read. Often questions are located at the beginning or the end of chapters. If authors do not include questions, you can make up your own by putting question words in front of headings and subheadings.

The fourth Ready strategy is to set your study length. This involves deciding how many pages you plan to read, as well as planning the length of your study sessions. A study/break ratio of 50:10:50 is recommended. Proper planning should help you eliminate wasted time and effort.

The fifth Ready strategy is to place Control □'s. Use the information you learned in the previous strategies about the chapter assignment and about your readiness for reading to select stopping places. Put Control □'s in these places to serve later as testing points while you are reading.

Review Questions

1. What does each letter of the acronym **SELF** stand for? Which of the areas of SELF do you feel need the most attention from you when you study? Why?

2. Explain the noisy-party phenomenon.

3. How can you still study effectively if you are emotionally upset? Give specific examples.

4. Why is some material more difficult to read? Name two strategies you can use to improve your comprehension when the material is difficult.

5. Discuss how your physical health affects your success in reading.

6. Why is taking a 10-minute break from studying a good idea? What caution should be observed when you take a study break?

7. Which parts of a textbook chapter do you usually look at when you preview? What else do you plan to notice or to do the next time you preview a chapter?

8. How can you create an interest in a subject you find boring?

9. When reading a textbook chapter, when should you look at the questions if they are furnished for you? How can you create questions if none exist? Explain your answers.

10. What are three benefits of placing Control □'s? Which of the three do you feel you need the most? Why?

Metacognitive Insights

Now that you have completed the first stage in BICUM and have tried several strategies, it is important that you record the metacognitive information you have learned. Try to include ideas in each of the three areas of metacognition: self-awareness, strategy awareness, and task awareness. Complete the following sentences, then use the blank lines to add more information as you gain more insights.

1. The time of day I study best is _____ because _____

   _____

   _____

2. Textbooks are hard for me when they _____

   _____

   _____

3. If I am worried about something when I try to study, I _____

   _____

   _____

4. Previewing a chapter helps me because _____

   _____

   _____

ADDITIONAL INSIGHTS

_____

_____

_____

_____

_____

_____

_____

Read

- Be Active
- Stop at ❏'s and Test Understanding

Yes, I do understand

- Determine key information

- Predict test questions

- Mark & highlight text

No, I don't understand

- Use fix-up strategies
1. Reread
2. Read ahead
3. Define unfamiliar words
4. Read out loud
5. Mark with "?" to clear up later

Continue to next ❏

3 READING FOR MEANING

When you read, read! Too many students just half read. . . . The art of memory is the art of understanding."

—*Roscoe Pound, Dean Emeritus*
Harvard Law School

The second stage in BICUM, *Read*, emphasizes the sentence *Reading is reading only when meaning is coming through*. Especially with college textbooks, half reading will not bring the desired results. To remember textbook information, understanding the material is essential.

Reading textbooks is one of the toughest tasks facing college students not only because of the difficulty of the material but also because of the amount of required reading. Understanding these books requires specific skills that usually are not taught in high school. To read college textbooks successfully, you must stay focused and correctly identify the most important information the author discusses in each chapter.

Textbooks also have the added challenge of more difficult vocabulary and very complex sentence structure. Reading college texts is not like reading novels or magazines. You must be active, thinking deeply as you read, considering the ideas and deciding how they relate to other ideas in the chapter and to your background knowledge. In short, you must actively search for meaning as you read.

Be Active

Reading is sometimes viewed as a passive process. Most likely you have had the experience of reading in a study environment not conducive to learning. Sometimes you read without marking anything, or being involved with the text.

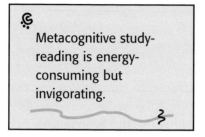

Metacognitive study-reading is energy-consuming but invigorating.

This is fine if you are reading magazines, newspapers, or novels for pleasure. However, reading textbooks should be anything but a passive experience. Successfully reading textbooks can sometimes be almost as exhausting as physical labor. Metacognitive study-reading is both energy-consuming and invigorating. It is a time to consciously search for meaning. To be an active reader, try the following:

1. **"Talking" with textbook authors** as you read is one way to get involved. Try mentally discussing the contents of the textbook chapter with the author. Picture him/her as a friend sitting beside you and discussing the subject you are reading. As you read, comment on the ideas that appeal to you. For example, you might say, "That's an intriguing concept," or "How surprising, I never knew that before." Likewise, question points about which you disagree with the author. You might say something similar to this: "I'm not sure that I agree with you. You are going to have to back up that statement." In short, mentally conversing with textbook authors helps move you from being a passive to an active learner.

2. Another way to read actively is to **visualize the information** you are covering. See yourself conducting the experiments, combining the chemicals, fighting in the battles, or repairing the automobiles. Picture yourself as a major participant in the events you are reading about. See, feel, taste, hear, and smell what you think the people in the texts are experiencing. Researchers have found that retention of information improved when subjects consciously created mental pictures. They also confirm that most people have excellent memory for pictures and picture-evoking words. Therefore, the more vividly you "paint" your mental pictures, the more likely you are to understand and remember what you read.

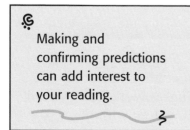

Making and confirming predictions can add interest to your reading.

3. **Making and confirming predictions** can add interest to your reading. Many students make it a personal challenge to "second guess" the author, to predict how concepts will be explained or will be developed. As you read, you can learn to anticipate

what might logically follow. You already began this process in the *Ready* stage (in Chapter 2). Furthermore, drawing on experience and background knowledge, you can make educated guesses about a logical order for the information to come. As you continue to read, your predictions will either be verified or found to be inaccurate. If you predicted correctly, compliment yourself; this is one indication that you are becoming a more proficient reader. Accurate predictions indicate that your background knowledge was adequate and your reasoning sound.

4. **Searching for answers to questions** can also prevent passive reading. Recall that during the *Ready* stage, you were instructed to read over the questions in your textbook or to create questions of your own. This technique prepared your mind for new information. Now as you go through the chapter, actively look for the answers to those questions. Some students describe this answer-hunting process as being similar to a treasure hunt. They explain that finding answers is like locating clues en route to a desired location. Actually, finding the answers to questions that have been provided or created will often provide you with the information that the author and your instructor consider to be most important.

5. **Pacing yourself with a pencil** as you read is an active reading technique that can help you both stay focused and read faster. In addition, increasing your pace or fluency often increases your comprehension as well. The physical movements involved in drawing your pencil across the lines of print tend to improve concentration, keeping your mind alert. Use a pencil to help focus your eyes on the words and move across and down the paper in a sweeping, flowing manner. Try this pacing strategy using the following steps. (Note: These steps work best when you have previewed the material you want to read.)

   • Place your pencil on the first line of print about 1 inch after the beginning of the material.

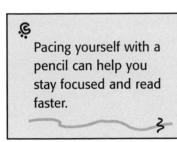

Pacing yourself with a pencil can help you stay focused and read faster.

- Move it across a line to about 1 inch before the right edge of the print.

- Swing back to the next line 1 inch from the left edge.

- Again move across the page to 1 inch before the end of this line.

Continue this sweeping movement back and forth, using your pencil as a focal point. Do not worry about the words on the edges of the lines. Your eyes have **peripheral vision,** the ability to see words or images on either side of a focal point. Most people can comfortably see about ½ to 1 inch around the point where they focus their eyes. In Figure 3.1, vertical lines demonstrate the point where most people can focus and still see the words on either side of the line. Some students find it necessary to draw these lines in their textbooks when first learning this technique.

Move your pencil in a sweeping action under each line of print, but within the vertical lines. Sweep back quickly to the next line. Push yourself to consciously increase your speed. When you first begin using this technique, your comprehension may decrease, but with practice it usually returns to previous levels.

Try reading the following paragraph using your pencil as a pacer. Read between the vertical lines allowing your peripheral vision to pick up the words on the edges.

> Reading can be addicting; the more you do it, the more you enjoy it. Few activities offer more excitement and open up as many opportunities and experiences as can reading. Once you get involved in an intriguing novel, it is difficult to put it down. You can unknowingly let chores go undone and allow your work to pile up. However, you may not "be able" to quit reading until you know how the book ends.

FIGURE 3.1 SAMPLE PARAGRAPH FOR PACING

How did it go? Did you understand what you read? Did your peripheral vision pick up the words outside the lines? Did your speed increase? Although this technique seems to work well for some students, others need more practice.

6. **Read in meaningful units or clusters.** As you pace yourself, avoid pointing to individual words and reading them separately. Rather, keep your pencil

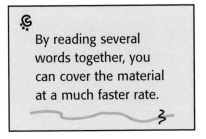

By reading several words together, you can cover the material at a much faster rate.

moving, reading groups of words in meaningful units. Practice this by reading the paragraph in Figure 3.2, which is divided into thought units. By reading several words together, you will be able to cover the material at a much faster rate.

Some people   keep a book   on a bedtime table   and pick it up each evening   to read for ten minutes.   They find that reading relaxes them. After they have read   a few pages   they sleep much better.

FIGURE 3.2 THOUGHT UNITS OR CLUSTERS

A final important note about active reading is the simple but powerful technique of intentionally increasing your speed and understanding. When you push yourself to read faster, you are less likely to get lost in the details because the ideas are coming into your mind more quickly and you are more likely to see the overall picture. MTA 3.1 will help you to develop the skills that were presented in this section.

Stop at □'s & Test Understanding

The previous chapter introduced the strategy of placing Control □'s. This techniques gives you a great opportunity to assess how much you learned from your reading. To do this, ask yourself, "Did I really understand what I just read?" If you did understand, you will be able to *paraphrase*, or put the information into your own words. This is necessary because it is possible to simply repeat ideas without truly understanding them. If you are studying in a place where talking would not disturb others, try to paraphrase this information out loud. As you attempt to vocalize ideas, you will more readily detect any areas that are confusing to you. Another reason to talk out loud is because you can remember your own voice more readily than your thoughts alone. However, if you are not fortunate enough to be in a private study area, just reviewing the material silently in your mind should be adequate. Remember though, the real test of comprehension is to be able to distinguish between

---

METACOGNITIVE TRAINING ACTIVITY
Be Active
·~· MTA 3.1 ·~·

⅗ DIRECTIONS:

Select one of the six strategies listed in this chapter under the
   Be Active section.

Actively read a three- to four-page section in one of your textbooks
   using the strategy you chose. (Ask your instructor for an
   alternative assignment if you do not have a text from another
   college course.)

Number your responses to the following items.

1. Name the strategy you chose.

2. List the title of the textbook chapter and the pages you read.

3. Describe your experience using this strategy, and tell how it
   affected your reading.

4. Will you use this strategy again? Why or why not?

5. Self grade _____% and brief justification.

---

ideas and know which ones can be ignored and which ones
are essential to retain for future study.

The next strategies you use will depend on how
successfully you understand the material that you read and
paraphrase. As you read, you will follow the instructions for
either "Yes, I do understand" or "No, I do not understand."
Remember that comprehension is crucial. Moving ahead
when you do not comprehend the material is a waste of
time. If you recognize a lack of understanding, take a few
minutes to use fix-up strategies before you continue. These
five strategies will be discussed later in this chapter. By
completing MTA 3.2, you will learn how to stay focused
while reading and avoid moving on without understanding.

> ℘
> Use fix-up strategies
> to get back on track
> before you continue.

METACOGNITIVE TRAINING ACTIVITY
Using Control □'s
·ᴣ· MTA 3.2 ·ᴣ·

ᴣ DIRECTIONS:

Preview the next assigned chapter from one of your course texts. (Ask your instructor for an alternative assignment if you are not taking another college course.)

Complete the SELF inventory to decide how ready you are to learn and how difficult the material seems.

Place Control □'s in the text with a pen or pencil *before* you beginning reading the assignment.

Read the chapter, stopping at your □'s to test your understanding.

If you are able to paraphrase the information, then selectively mark and/or annotate the section you have just read.

If you can't paraphrase what you have read, use one or more of the five fix-up strategies to gain understanding before continuing to read.

After reading the chapter, respond to the following items.

NOTE: For grading purposes your instructor may ask you to provide a copy of the chapter you used for the assignment.

1. List the name of the course, text, and chapter you used for this assignment.

2. Briefly describe what you did when you came to each Control □.

3. Did your concentration improve as a result of using Control □'s? Why or why not?

4. Did you notice an improvement in your understanding of the material from using this technique? Explain.

5. If you use this method again, list any changes you would make to be more effective. If you would not make any changes, explain why.

6. Self grade _____% and brief justification.

Yes, I Do Understand

As you are reading, part of the metacognitive process is to ask yourself, "Am I understanding what I am reading?" If the answer to this question is yes, then there are still steps that you need to take to actually learn the material. It is not only essential to understand what you are reading but it is important to be able to identify the key information to remember when you read. A discussion of how to determine which information is important enough to be learned will follow.

Determine Key Information

Topics, main ideas, and major supporting details usually comprise the key information you are expected to master. Students who can quickly and accurately identify this crucial information and distinguish it from minor details and introductory material can often reduce their study time, improve their test scores, and increase their retention of the most important information.

Identify the Topic

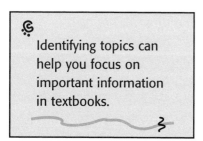

Identifying topics can help you focus on important information in textbooks.

One way to find meaning in what you read, particularly with difficult textbook material, is to identify the **topics,** or the subjects discussed in paragraphs. Skillfully identifying topics when you read can help you to focus on information that is important in the chapter.

Although this skill may appear easy or even unimportant to you, with time you will come to appreciate its benefits not only in reading but in other academic tasks as well. You will find that learning to determine precise topics has many benefits for thinking and writing. For instance, in courses where research projects and other papers are required, college professors usually expect their students to submit precise topics before major research and/or writing begins. Students who are unable to

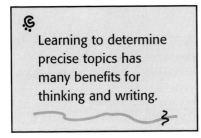

Learning to determine precise topics has many benefits for thinking and writing.

appropriately construct precise topics find that it is difficult to begin. If they choose a topic that is too general, they are unable to limit their research to the required number of pages. Those students who choose a topic that is too narrow are unable to find enough information and/or sources to adequately address the issue.

The topic of a paragraph is a description of its contents and can usually be expressed in a few words or in a phrase. Every paragraph has a topic because every paragraph is *about* something or someone. Therefore, to find the topic, ask yourself the following question:

Who or what is this paragraph about?

The previous question is natural to ask about things of interest. For example, when you join a group of friends having a discussion, you might ask, "What are you talking about?" In addition, it is not uncommon to wonder what a new movie or novel is it about when you first hear the title. In these examples, your mind is searching for further meaning and attempting to organize it according to your background knowledge. Therefore, asking yourself questions can also become an automatic part of your reading.

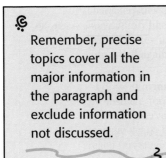

Remember, precise topics cover all the major information in the paragraph and exclude information not discussed.

FIND A PRECISE TOPIC   Those students who are able to ask good questions, can then develop and convey clear topics which follow the author's train of thought. Their thinking becomes more discriminating and less careless and inaccurate. In order for this kind of critical thinking to occur, the topics you create should be *precise*. This means they must be specific enough to exclude ideas not discussed in a paragraph or section but general enough to include all or most of the information covered.

Authors often use general topics for their titles, as illustrated by the bold headings of the practice paragraphs that follow. Writers who are already familiar with the information they are presenting have the freedom to use general topics or titles. Readers, on the other hand, need to be able to identify precisely what they are reading about and also need to be able to convey their understanding to others. Learning to identify precise topics will also help you bring to a conscious level the process of gaining meaning and allow you to do it more quickly.

The section that follows will give you an idea of what is meant by determining precise topics. But, in order to gain a more complete understanding of topics, you will also need to read and understand the sections on main idea and major details.

To more easily identify topics, look for the following hints in paragraphs:

1. **Headings or titles** Notice that the following paragraphs entitled "The American Revolution" and "Computer Viruses" have bold headings. These give you a general starting place to decide what the paragraphs are about.

2. **Repeated words or references to key words** Also, notice words that relate to the headings by using repeated words, synonyms, or pronouns.

Read the following paragraph and write a precise topic on the line below the paragraph. As you read, also look for the hints mentioned above.

The American Revolution

The American Revolution was an accelerated evolution rather than an outright revolution in the sense of a radical or total change. It did not suddenly and violently overturn the entire political and social framework, as later occurred in the French and Russian revolutions. During the conflict itself people went on working and praying, marrying and playing. Most of them were not seriously disturbed by the actual fighting, and many of the more isolated communities scarcely knew that a war was going on.
—Bailey and Kennedy, *The American Pageant* (Rev.)

Precise Topic: _____

The paragraph on the American Revolution contains both of the hints for topics mentioned previously. There is a heading or title, and the word "revolution" is repeated several times. Also, other words throughout the paragraph are used almost as synonyms because they refer back to the American Revolution. These words are "the conflict," "actual fighting," and "war."

In the second sentence the word "it" also refers to the American Revolution. Using pronouns instead of continually repeating the subject is another way that authors emphasize topics without unnecessary repetition of key words. If you selected *the American Revolution* as the topic, you are not wrong, but your choice would be too general because it would cover anything even remotely related to the American Revolution. If, for instance, you entered that topic as a search on the Internet, you would likely access far more information than you could handle.

Possible topics that are more precise might include *the American Revolution: an accelerated evolution* or *reasons the American Revolution was not a total change.* Notice that these samples are **phrases,** not sentences. These topics do not contain verbs and are therefore not complete sentences. Topics should *not* be stated in complete sentences because sentences make a point and topics do not; they only name or describe what is being discussed.

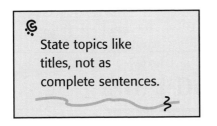

State topics like titles, not as complete sentences.

Further explanation and examples of the difference between topics and main ideas will be given later in this chapter. Learning to distinguish between these is great exercise for the mind. The ability to do it well is often a sign of well-developed critical thinking.

Think of the way most books, chapters, and sections are titled. These are examples of topics that authors are discussing. If titles or topics are clear and precise, your mind begins to focus more easily on the topic under discussion. If authors use general or misleading titles, sometimes your mind begins to go in one direction and you find that the material has a different slant. This is not only confusing; it actually wastes valuable study time. Since your mind naturally begins to search your memory for what you already know about different subjects, you may find yourself side-tracked by vague or misleading titles.

Starting with the obvious general topic of a paragraph is a good beginning, but skillful readers find that the more quickly and accurately they can narrow the focus to a more precise aspect of the general subject being discussed, the more efficient and effective they are in understanding what they are reading.

Some students find that it is helpful to think of this process as trying to create a perfect title for each paragraph.

When students practice accurately naming or describing what is being discussed in particular paragraphs or sections of writing, this process soon becomes almost second nature. They find that their minds begin to focus quickly and almost unconsciously on key information. In addition, retention can be enhanced because precise topics can serve as memory cues when recalling information for exams.

For example, if you created a precise topic for the previous paragraph on the American Revolution, such as *reasons the American Revolution was not a total change,* then key words in that topic would help you remember the important details given. As you tried to recall reasons why the American Revolution was not a total change, then facts or evidence like (1) it did not suddenly and violently overturn the entire political and social framework and (2) people went right on working, marrying, and playing would more easily come to mind.

Remembering just the general topic, the American Revolution, would not be as likely to trigger memory of important details since so much information relates to that broad topic. If topics are too general, then thinking regarding them is likely to be scattered rather than focused.

One way of determining precise topics and key information is to examine how all of the sentences and ideas in a paragraph relate to each other. When we can recognize what point the author is making about the topic, we are more likely to recognize other related information. The topic and the main idea serve as organizational structures around which major details may be organized.

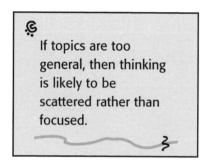

If topics are too general, then thinking is likely to be scattered rather than focused.

EXAMINE PARAGRAPHS CLOSELY   Since paragraphs are the building blocks of reading, examining paragraphs closely helps readers develop the comprehension skills necessary to generalize to longer selections, chapters, and books. In the following pages you will notice that some of the practice paragraphs are repeated. This has been intentional to help make the concepts easier to understand.

While most students have little difficulty following a story line, as in novels and other narrative material, they often experience difficulty reading college textbooks because most college texts are written to inform, rather that entertain. The information follows a different format or structure. Examining expository paragraphs will help you to realize that they often only contain a few essential components. Often the most information in the text paragraphs can be categorized as main ideas and major details, both of which are organized into various patterns.

To give you some additional practice in clarifying your thinking and understanding, read the following paragraph and write a precise topic on the line below the selection. Then read the explanation that follows to see if you were successful.

Computer Viruses

A computer virus is a program that resides, unknown to the computer user, on his or her hard or floppy disks, either damaging or destroying programs, files, and data. This may entail regenerating mistakes, altering other programs, or erasing entire memory banks. Viruses do not discriminate; they affect personal computers as well as computer systems and networks.

Precise Topic: _____

A precise topic or title for this paragraph could be *the definition and effects of computer viruses* or *what computer viruses are and what they do*. Of course other possibilities exist, but either of these topics is general enough to cover all the important information in the paragraph, yet precise enough to describe what this paragraph contains.

Notice that the word "computers" by itself would be too general as a topic; it would cover much more than what is contained in the paragraph. Buying computers, selling computers, changes in computers, problems with computers, and so forth could all be included under the general topic of "computers." That is why choosing one word like *computers* as the topic is not precise enough to clearly identify what a paragraph is about.

Adding more precise words such as *definition* and *effects* to the author's general title of "Computer Viruses" helps cluster or categorize the other information given in this particular paragraph about the general topic of computers or computer viruses. By adding a few well-chosen words, the topic is narrowed and becomes more precise. Deciding which words are appropriate to add to the general topic requires examining and evaluating the point

> To decide which words are appropriate to add for a precise topic requires an examination of the main idea and major details.

being made about the topic and the major details given to support the point. In other words, this skill requires students to recognize not only (1) **who** or **what** the paragraph is about but also (2) the **point** being made and (3) the information given to **back up** the point.

This process requires a number of higher level thinking skills. As with the development of any other skill, persistence and practice are required to do it well. Students who expect the process to be very simple can become frustrated when they begin. However, if you practice persistently, you will develop skills that will enhance your reading for a lifetime.

The above paragraphs discussed the problems with topics that are too general, but being too specific is also problematic. For example, *viruses that affect personal computers* would be too specific for the paragraph that we have been discussing. This phrase or topic would not cover the parts of the paragraph that define computer viruses and describe their effects on systems and networks. Remember, precise topics cover *all* of the major information in the paragraph and exclude information not discussed.

Some students might be tempted to use words from the first sentence, which defines computer viruses, as their topic. Of course the definition of computer viruses is important for understanding the rest of the paragraph, but the definition alone would be too narrow because it does not cover the other major details given in the rest of the paragraph.

Remember that the topic is an important part of the main point or main idea. Think about the message of the paragraph and ask yourself what most of the sentences are talking about. The subject under discussion is the topic. The point being made about that topic will be the main idea.

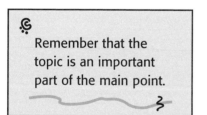

Remember that the topic is an important part of the main point.

Determine the Main Idea

The main point that the author makes about the subject or topic being discussed is often the most important information given in any paragraph. According to Smith (1997), many reading teachers feel that **understanding main ideas** is the most important reading skill you can

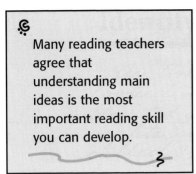

Many reading teachers agree that understanding main ideas is the most important reading skill you can develop.

develop. Recognizing main ideas serves as a means to help readers decide if the remaining information in a paragraph is of major or minor importance. That which directly supports the main idea is essential information; that which could be deleted or forgotten after initial reading is usually considered minor.

Authors sometimes state their main point in one sentence and then use additional information to back up or support this statement. In other paragraphs, however, the main ideas are suggested or implied by the details given. You should become proficient in recognizing stated main ideas and also inferring main ideas that are unstated or implied. This usually requires drawing conclusions from the details. Both kinds of main ideas will be discussed in the pages that follow.

LOCATE THE (STATED) MAIN IDEA   Although not all paragraphs have *stated* main ideas, including them in textbook passages is fairly common. Since main idea statements are the most important points authors make about topics, identifying them improves comprehension. To locate main ideas, ask one or both of the following questions:

> What point does the author make about the subject?
>
> What does the author want me to understand about the topic?

The answer to either of these questions is the main idea. It is sometimes referred to as an "umbrella" statement because it is a general sentence that "covers" the major information in the paragraph. The main idea does not have to cover introductions or all minor details, but it should be general enough to cover the major supporting details.

The main idea statement is also called the **topic sentence** because, it contains the topic of the passage. In addition, it may be referred to as the **main point** or **central idea.** However, no matter what it is called, the main idea must always be expressed *in a complete sentence.* Because the topic sentence makes a point, it cannot be stated in a phrase or as a question.

Read again the paragraph entitled "The American Revolution." This time ask yourself, "What main point does the author make about this topic?" Underline the directly stated main.

The American Revolution

The American Revolution was an accelerated evolution rather than an outright revolution in the sense of a radical or total change. It did not suddenly and violently overturn the entire political and social framework, as later occurred in the French and Russian revolutions. During the conflict itself people went on working and praying, marrying and playing. Most of them were not seriously disturbed by the actual fighting, and many of the more isolated communities scarcely knew that a war was going on.
—Bailey and Kennedy, *The American Pageant* (Rev.)

Did you choose the first sentence: "The American Revolution was an accelerated evolution rather than an outright revolution in the sense of a radical or total change"? If you did, you are right. This sentence contains the most important information the author wants you to know about the topic. It is also the only sentence that mentions the general topic, the American Revolution. The rest of the paragraph explains that point. Placing the main idea in the first sentence is a frequent practice and is probably the most common place to find the main idea.

A triangle with the wide part at the top graphically represents this location of a main idea. The main idea is followed by more specific information, called supporting details.

Main Idea

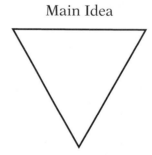

Read the following paragraph, locate the directly stated main idea, and underline it.

In the seventeenth century, sailors at sea frequently suffered from muscle weakness and unexplained bleeding. Often this disease proved fatal until it was discovered that sailors who ate oranges or lemons either did not get sick or else suffered from a milder form of the disease. As a result, British navy officials passed a law requiring that every ship provide oranges and lemons for the crew. By accident, the navy had discovered that these citrus fruits which contained vitamin C prevented the disease we now know as scurvy.

—From Flemming, *Reading for Success*

In the previous paragraph the last sentence contains the main idea: *By accident, the navy had discovered that these citrus fruits which contained vitamin C prevented the disease we now know as scurvy.* This sentence is the main point the author wants you to understand about the topic, which could be either *preventing scurvy with citrus fruits* or *the navy's discovery of how to prevent scurvy.* The shape that illustrates paragraphs with the main idea as the final sentence is a triangle with the wide part at the bottom. The author leads up to the point by giving you specific details before stating the main idea. The last sentence is usually the second most common place for directly stated main ideas or topic sentences to be located.

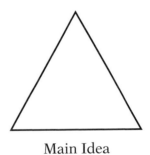

Main Idea

In the following exercises you will see that a stated main idea can be located anywhere in the paragraph. Locate the directly stated main idea in the paragraph below and underline it.

Some people believe that lie detectors should be used to determine the guilt or innocence of accused persons. They believe that these machines accurately detect persons who are not telling the truth. In reality, lie detectors are not foolproof because they can very easily make mistakes. For example, some people become anxious when they are hooked up to the machines. Their anxiety is recorded as lying even if they are telling the truth. Other people, who are lying, have become so good at "making up stories" that they show no emotion.

Did you select a sentence in the middle of the paragraph? That is where the main point is located. The main idea or topic sentence is *In reality, lie detectors are not foolproof because they can very easily make mistakes.* The words "in reality" at the beginning of the main idea sentence are indicators or signals given by the author that an important point is being made. Notice that this main idea sentence also contains the general topic, which is *lie detectors*.

A more precise topic for this paragraph might be *causes for lie detectors not being foolproof.* You may have noticed the word *causes* in the topic and you may be wondering why that word is being used. If you examine the details given after the main idea, *causes* is a word that categorizes or labels those details about how people experiencing anxiety or how practiced liars can "fool" a lie detector.

A diamond shape illustrates the location of this main idea because the author gives specific details or facts before and after stating his/her point.

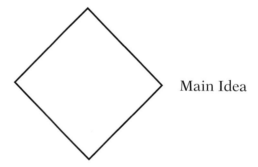

Main Idea

Although a stated main idea may be located anywhere throughout the paragraph, be sure to check the beginning and final sentences first. Remember these are the most common locations for this important information when it is directly stated in one sentence. Authors also frequently state the main idea in both the first and the last sentence. The last sentence is often a restatement of the first, and you must decide which of these sentences states the point more clearly or if combining the two is necessary. This restatement of the main idea is illustrated by an "hourglass" shape.

Main Idea

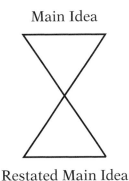

Restated Main Idea

In MTA 3.3 (p. 80) you will use paragraphs that are provided in Appendix A to see how proficient you are at determining the directly stated main ideas and topics.

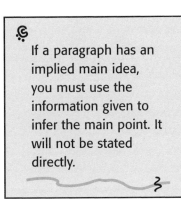

If a paragraph has an implied main idea, you must use the information given to infer the main point. It will not be stated directly.

FORMULATE THE IMPLIED MAIN IDEA   Even though all paragraphs have topics, not all paragraphs have directly stated main ideas. Sometimes, the main ideas are unstated, or **implied.** Your task in these paragraphs is to use the information given to make educated guesses about the author's point, or to *infer* the main ideas. In other words, you must determine the author's main idea yourself. This means that you must formulate or create the point the author is making about the topic and state it in a complete sentence.

There are several common ways to formulate implied main ideas. For example, sometimes you may be able to simply combine two sentences. When that does not sufficiently make the author's point, then try combining some of your words with the author's ideas to convey his/her message. This usually requires drawing conclusions from the details given in the paragraph and stating the main idea mostly in your own words. Realize that whatever method you use when formulating a main idea, you must stay with the point the author makes and not get side-tracked with your own ideas and/or opinions.

When writing an implied main idea, you must stay with the point the author is making.

The following paragraph does not have a stated main idea. See if you can infer what the author wants you to know about the topic by using one of the methods mentioned above to create your own topic sentence. Write your inferred main idea on the lines below the selection.

METACOGNITIVE TRAINING ACTIVITY
Identify Topics and Main Ideas
·~· MTA 3.3 ·~·

⸘ DIRECTIONS:

Go to the Appendix A Practice Paragraphs, and use paragraphs 3 and 7. Label them by paragraph number.

Record the number of each item below and give complete responses.

1. Identify the **directly stated main idea** for each paragraph. Write them out so that you and the instructor can evaluate whether your choice is valid or note. To do this, use the following criteria:

   ▶ Is the main idea general enough to cover all of the major details?
   ▶ Does it contain the topic being discussed?
   ▶ Is the main idea a complete sentence?
   ▶ Is it making the author's point?

2. Identify a **precise topic** for each paragraph by circling words in the main idea or topic sentence.

3. Self grade _____% and brief justification.

Losing a spouse has been listed as one of the most stressful events in a person's life, and the question is sometimes asked whether men or women adjust more easily to this loss. Although widows are more likely to suffer financial setbacks than widowers, they usually have more close friends to provide emotional support. In addition, adult children tend to rally more around the mother than the father when a parent dies.

Main Idea _____

_____

_____

The *topic* of this paragraph could be "widows adjusting more easily to the loss of a spouse than widowers or gender differences in adjusting to the loss of a spouse. Even though these phrases are long and may look like sentences, they are not complete thoughts and therefore do not make a point. The reader cannot be certain of the author's point from the phrases given above because the author might have said something like, "There are no gender differences in the adjustment to the loss of a spouse." Of course if that were the case, the supporting details would have to be changed as well to back up that point.

The **implied main idea** that the author is making could be one of the following sentences:

> Widows adjust more easily to the loss of a spouse than widowers.

> or

> Gender differences exist in adjusting to the loss of a spouse.

Sometimes by rearranging words in a phrase or a dependent clause, it is possible to create a sentence. In the examples of the main ideas given above, the word *adjust* can be used as a verb in the main idea sentence. By careful rearrangement of the words, instead of an indefinite idea, a strong conclusion is reached that leaves no doubt in the reader's mind about the point being made.

You do not have to use the same words as the sentences above, but you must state the same point that the author makes about the topic. The main idea will be supported by the major details. The author gives two major supports to guide you in making this inference: (1) *Widows have more supportive friends*, and (2) *Adult children tend to rally more around the mother than the father*. These sentences help you understand why widows or women adjust more easily to the loss of a spouse than widowers or men.

Notice that either of the above main ideas answers the question about whether men or women adjust more easily to the loss of spouse. A frequent technique used by authors is to pose a question, usually in the introduction, and then answer the question to make their point. Not only do questions help create interest in what is being read, but questions will often lead readers to the author's point.

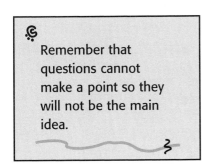

Remember that questions cannot make a point so they will not be the main idea.

Remember that questions themselves cannot make a point, but they are still useful to notice because they will often contain the subject matter or topic and they can also help facilitate the reader's search for meaning.

The shape that illustrates paragraphs that do not have stated main ideas is a rectangle. No one sentence in the paragraph is general enough to cover the rest of the ideas. All of the sentences must be considered together to discover the point or the main idea.

No Stated Main Idea

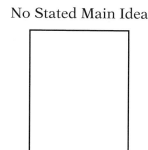

Implied main ideas are usually a little more challenging for students to determine; you will find that it gets easier with practice. Begin by working through MTA 3.4 to help you develop this important skill.

Find the Major Supporting Details

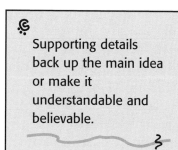

Supporting details back up the main idea or make it understandable and believable.

Supporting details are the items of information that back up the main idea or make it understandable and believable. For instance, the important details present such things as reasons, examples, facts, and steps that explain the point the author is making about the subject. In most expository or informational material, such as that found in the majority of textbooks, there are two kinds of supporting details: major and minor.

As the name implies, major details are the more important ones. Their primary function is to support the main idea, like legs on a table. Without their support readers are less likely to believe or accept the main point. Major details will usually be more general than minor ones. If major details are followed by very specific information

---

METACOGNITIVE TRAINING ACTIVITY
Write Implied Main Ideas
·ᴣ· MTA 3.4 ·ᴣ·

ᴣ DIRECTIONS:
The following MTA requires you to write implied main ideas (IMI). Go
   to Appendix A, and use paragraphs 2 and 9 for the exercise.
List the paragraph number for each IMI.

1. Write an implied main idea for each paragraph. You may use a
   combination of your own words and those used by the author.

2. Choose words that would make a good topic or title and circle
   them in your implied main idea.

3. Is it easier for you to find the topic or the main idea first?

There are the three checks, listed below, for validating main ideas.
   Use them to evaluate your main ideas.

Check #1 Is each main idea a complete sentence that makes the
   author's definite point?
Check #2 Did each main idea contain words that you could circle as
   the topic or title?
Check #3 Is each main idea general enough to cover all of the major
   supporting details?

4. Self grade _____% and brief justification.

> **Main ideas and major details are the core of reading.**

that helps you to understand them more precisely, that information will most likely be minor details.

Along with main ideas, major details are the core of reading. The information found in main ideas and major details will usually appear on college exams and will most often be the information college students will be expected to retain from semester to semester.

Being able to correctly identify main ideas and major supporting details will also allow readers to effectively use the marking techniques discussed in chapter 3 and reduction techniques discussed in chapter 4. By focusing on the most important information, students can reduce the amount of information they are trying to learn and remember. They will be able to use this key information to construct effective review sheets and study tools instead of trying to reread entire chapters for exams. Rereading the entire chapter is one of the most inefficient methods of study.

Correctly identifying authors' main points is the key to finding major details, and finding major details is the surest way to verify authors' points. These work hand-in-hand to guide readers to a clear understanding of what they are reading.

Reread the paragraph that follows on the American Revolution, but this time pick out the major supporting details. Number and underline the major supports in the paragraph. The details that you choose must support the main idea stated in the first sentence.

> The American Revolution was an accelerated evolution rather than outright revolution in the sense of a radical or total change. It did not suddenly and violently overturn the entire political and social framework, as later occurred in the French and Russian revolutions. During the conflict itself people went on working and praying, marrying and playing. Most of them were not seriously disturbed by the actual fighting, and many of the more isolated communities scarcely knew that a war was going on.
> —*Bailey and Kennedy, The American Pageant* (Rev.)

Topic: the American Revolution: not an outright revolution

Main Idea: The American Revolution was not a revolution in the sense of a radical or total change.

Did you find the following four **major details**? (1) *It did not suddenly and violently overturn the entire political and social framework.* (2) *People went on working, praying, marrying and playing.* (3) *Most people were not seriously disturbed by the actual fighting.* (4) *Many of the more isolated communities scarcely knew that a war was going on.*

As you can see, the major supporting details make the main idea statement believable. After reading these supports, it is easy to understand why the author stated that the American Revolution did not involve radical or total change.

Notice that each of the major details gives a distinctive piece of information to back up the point made in the first sentence. For example, the fact that the American

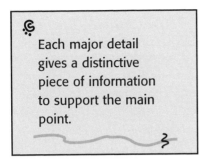

Each major detail gives a distinctive piece of information to support the main point.

Revolution was not a violent overturn of the entire American political and social framework is significantly different from the fact that during the revolution many isolated communities scarcely knew that a war was going on. In a day of modern communication, that detail seems almost unimaginable. Each of these major details adds important information to your understanding of why the American Revolution was not a revolution in the usual sense.

MINOR DETAILS   The paragraph on the American Revolution contains very few, if any, minor details. One minor detail might be the specific reference to the French and Russian revolutions as a contrast to the American Revolution. This reference clarifies the first major detail, or tells you that the American Revolution was not as sudden and violent as some revolutions have been.

Minor details, as their name implies, are less important than major details, but they still serve a useful purpose to explain and clarify major details, usually by giving very specific examples. Minor details often add "color" and interest to writing by appealing to your senses and by giving information that helps you visualize or picture in your mind what you are reading.

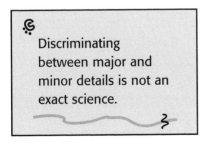

Minor details serve a useful purpose to explain and clarify major details and to add "color" and interest to writing.

Minor details, however, can sometimes be omitted from paragraphs, and the main idea will still be clear and believable. It is also important to note that minor details seldom appear on college exams. By omitting the review of minor details when mastering course material, students will find that they usually retain more of the course essentials.

Without being in the position of the writer, it is sometimes very difficult to accurately determine where major details end and minor ones begin. In fact, discriminating between major and minor details is not an exact science. However, learning to select the most important information is a vital skill for decreasing study time and improving test scores. It is a necessary step toward reducing and remembering the key information in college texts.

You might wish to include the minor detail about the French and Russian revolutions discussed in the previous paragraph with your major details. In this particular case there is little to guide you about whether the author intended this detail to be major or minor, so it would be

Discriminating between major and minor details is not an exact science.

your choice whether or not to include it with the major detail it supports.

Both kinds of details serve a useful purpose in writing and reading. When in doubt, include more rather than less. Teachers will not penalize you for knowing too much. Some general guidelines for identifying minor details, however, may be helpful.

As a general rule, minor details are usually much more specific than major ones. They often give very precise examples about something mentioned earlier. Introductory quotes, questions, or stories that are intended to catch the reader's attention are usually included in the minor detail category. These are much like the personal anecdotes or jokes some instructors use to begin their lectures. Just as you would not take notes on these stories or jokes, or at least not expect them to appear on course exams, neither would you be wise to focus on these kinds of minor details in your textbook study.

MAJOR VERSUS MINOR DETAILS   To give you some experience in discriminating between major and minor details, read the following selection entitled "Mental Imagery." It has been annotated for you as a model.

As you read, notice the markings or annotations in the selection and in the margin. Notice the labeled main idea (MI), the major details that have been numbered and underlined, and the minor details that have been enclosed in parentheses. Some of the information is unmarked because it is difficult to strictly categorize all information. This method of marking is a useful strategy when first learning how to distinguish between these two kinds of details, but may not be the most practical for reading large amounts of material. It can be helpful when information is difficult to understand and important to remember. Other ways of marking essential ideas will be discussed later in the chapter in the section on marking and highlighting text (pp. 91–94).

> As a general rule, minor details are usually much more specific than major ones.

Mental Imagery

Understanding how your mind can create and use mental imagery has several practical applications in enjoying and remembering what you read. First of all, the fact that your mind is capable of creating mental pictures, even in color, enhances your ability

MI

to mentally "see" and enjoy what you are reading. (For instance, suppose you are reading a novel that describes a beautiful mountain scene. It is possible to "see" in your mind the quaking aspens, to "hear" the movement of the wind through the leaves, and to "smell" the evergreens nearby.)

2. Another reason for being aware of mental imagery is to mentally recreate the pictures you draw on your study cards and/or in the margins of your texts to help you understand and remember difficult textbook concepts. For example, when you are trying to learn and remember the definitions of new terms, you can create visuals that represent the definitions you are trying to learn. Later, while trying to remember the definitions of these terms, you can mentally visualize the pictures you drew which will cue your memory with the concept you are trying to remember. (Think, for instance, of a picture to help you remember the word philanthropist. One student suggested a heart shape with a $ in the center of it. The meaning of that word is conveyed by the heart and the $ because philanthropists love people and typically give them money.)

MI Restated

As you are reviewing for exams and especially while you are taking them, you can visualize or get a mental image of the pictures you have created, either in your mind or on paper, to more readily see and remember the information you have read.

Did you notice that the main idea was stated in the first sentence and restated as a conclusion in the last one? The passage is about *the practical applications for creating mental imagery to enjoy and remember what you read,* and all of those topic words can be found in the first sentence. When you try to determine which details give direct support for this point, it is useful to identify the major reasons or practical applications for creating mental images: to enjoy and remember what you read.

In the second paragraph, the information that is not underlined, following the words *for example,* could be considered either part of the major detail or a minor one, or it could be seen as a transition between the two. This is an example of how complex reading can be. Since it is

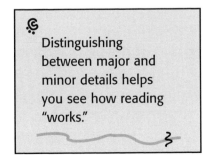

Distinguishing between major and minor details helps you see how reading "works."

impossible to strictly categorize paragraph information in every instance, you as a reader must decide what you wish to focus on in your textbook study. Having some experience with major and minor details and knowing some guidelines for distinguishing between them, however, can raise your level of awareness and help you begin to notice how reading "works."

The very specific examples included in the parentheses are clearly minor details. They serve a useful purpose to illustrate the point being supported. You might even remember them when trying to recall some reasons for creating mental images. It is highly unlikely that an instructor would expect you to remember the very specific details on an exam. However, a professor might, in this case, expect you to know that using mental images helps you to enjoy and remember what you have read.

Try marking the following selection entitled "Knowing the Ropes in College" by using the system shown on pages 86–87. Then read the explanation that follows to see if you were successful.

Knowing the Ropes in College

Do I need to take notes in this class? Does attendance count? Will my instructors accept late work? All of these questions are typical of those asked by beginning college students. Knowing what professors expect can sometimes make or break students in college.

Major blunders on assignments can be disastrous. A case in point might be when a student hands in a paper without correcting spelling and grammar errors and then wonders why he/she receives a poor grade. Another student might fail to follow assignment instructions and be upset when the teacher will not allow the assignment to be redone.

Missing deadlines is another source of student failure. A student may try to take a test after the posted deadline and discover that the test is no longer available in the testing center. An inexperienced student may hand in a research paper a day late and be surprised when the instructor will not accept it.

Knowing the ropes in college, not just passing tests, can often mean the difference between success and failure. The sooner students learn what professors expect, the better their chances are for succeeding in college.

The main idea of this passage is stated several times in different ways. This is not unusual because writers usually want their readers to "get the point." *Knowing what professors expect can make or break students in college* is one way the main idea is stated. The last two sentences serves as a conclusion but also restate the main point in different words.

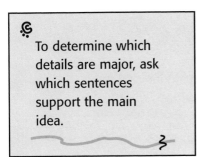

To determine which details are major, ask which sentences support the main idea.

To determine which details are major and support the main point, ask yourself which sentences back up the main idea and look for those details. For example, you could ask, "Which sentences give the expectations professors have that can make or break students in college?"

The two major kinds of expectations that professors have are that students will (1) avoid major blunders on assignments and (2) not miss course deadlines. Did you number and underline the sentences containing that information? These are the major details. Notice that the words "blunders," "assignments," and "deadlines" are all plurals, which means that more than one example of each of them may be given. They are also more specific than some words used in the main idea, such as a reference to professors' expectations. The very specific examples of assignment blunders and missed deadlines represent minor details. Did you put all of them in parentheses?

Another way to determine the main idea and verify that it is indeed the point, is to look at the details given and ask yourself what most of the information is talking about. Each of the details in "Knowing the Ropes in College" seems to be discussing problems that students may have in college if they do not know what their professors expect. By adding up these details or analyzing what they have in common, it is possible to reach the conclusion that it is important to meet professors' expectations to be successful in college.

In MTA 3.5 that follows, you will use some familiar paragraphs to continue your practice of locating key information.

METACOGNITIVE TRAINING ACTIVITY
Find Major Supporting Details
·¿· MTA 3.5 ·¿·

⸮ DIRECTIONS:

Use paragraphs 3 and 7 from Appendix A for this assignment.
Identify the major details, and number and underline them in the
    paragraph.
Make sure to answer the following questions for both of the
    paragraphs and to organize your responses so that it is clear
    which questions go with each paragraph.

---

1. Write the major supporting details, paraphrasing them
   whenever possible.

2. What do the major details answer: who, what, where, why,
   when, or how?

3. How do you distinguish between major and minor supporting
   details?

4. Self grade _____% and brief justification.

Predict Test Questions

One of the most important metacognitive skills you can gain is that of learning to predict test questions. As you stop at a control box, ask yourself which parts of the section you just read will be important enough to commit to memory. One way to determine that may be to notice the amount of space that the author used to develop a concept. Also, it usually helps to make connections between your reading and the class lectures. Note those ideas from your text that the professor also discusses and emphasizes. Listen for verbal cues such as, "this is important information," or "you should pay careful attention as I explain the following points, covered on pages . . ." As you practice anticipating what will be on exams, you can become very proficient.

A reading and study skills instructor, Eldon McMurray, advises his students to mark information on which they are likely to be tested with a "**T**". This symbol can also represent information to be transferred to cue cards and ideas teachers consider to be important. Using this technique, one of his students was able to accurately predict, and rehearse with her cue cards, 91 out of the 100 questions on her final exam.

The more you can learn to think like a teacher, the more skillful you will be at accurately predicting and practicing test questions, resulting in raised test scores and higher grades. As Eldon McMurray tells his students, this will be another indication for you that "you can become your own best teacher."

Mark & Highlight Text

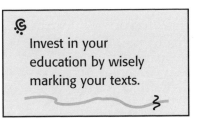

Invest in your education by wisely marking your texts.

Do not hesitate to write in your textbooks. They are the "tools of the trade" for students. Many college bookstores buy back books that have been marked and highlighted at the same used-book rate as those that are unmarked. Even if your bookstore does not have this policy, invest in your education by marking your texts. Effective marking will improve your memory of textbook material, and you will likely decide that it is worth the few dollars you might lose in book resale. The money that you pay for your textbooks is not one of the greater expenses of college. Nist and Simpson (1988) have demonstrated that use of underlining and marginal annotations help students improve their test performance. Resist the temptation to mark or highlight as you read. If you mark before you have a clear understanding, you might emphasize the wrong information or mark too much. Research shows that either of these situations actually interferes with memory. In fact, according to Peterson (1992) students who do not mark their textbook at all do better than those who mark them indiscriminately. If you wait until you have stopped at your Control □'s to paraphrase and check your understanding before you begin marking, you will be much more likely to mark constructively.

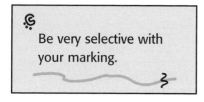

Be very selective with your marking.

Be very selective with your marking. Generally, you will want to mark or highlight only fifteen to twenty-five percent of the text. Emphasize only the material that is essential to remember. Before you can use memory techniques, it is vital that you are first able to select the most important information and the details you can forget.

To help you decide which information is essential to mark and remember, you must consider a number of factors. One consideration is the college course or discipline. Each kind of course may have its own peculiar emphasis. For example, some history courses stress names, dates, and important events. Philosophy and some of the social sciences courses will likely stress principles and concepts with broader application. Science courses usually require knowledge of basic facts and information before larger concepts can be mastered.

Another factor to consider when marking the text is discover what individual teachers consider important. Instructors vary in what they emphasize. Some may stress material covered in texts more heavily than lecture material. This puts a greater burden on you to learn the information more independently. It is sometimes necessary for you to "get a feel for" what these individual professors will expect you to learn. You may accomplish this by doing such things as reviewing the first exam, listening for lecture clues, and asking good questions about what to expect on exams, etc.

A sample of marked text is shown in Figure 3.3. Use what you like from this marking system and add to it to create your own techniques that you can use consistently in marking textbooks. This is only one system of marking key information.

Some college courses focus heavily on vocabulary and concept development. In many entry-level courses learning the "language" or the vocabulary of a particular discipline, is a major focus in beginning to understand that discipline. Identifying and correctly marking important terminology are important steps in mastering essential information.

Some students suggest underlining and annotating the text with a pencil when they first read the material. When they review the material, they also highlight only the things that they were unable to remember from their first reading. This technique is valuable because color makes the material easier to visualize mentally.

Piaget's Theory of Cognitive Development

Overall MI Main Idea [

Perhaps the most widely accepted theory of cognitive development was espoused by Jean Piaget. He purported that children world wide develop in a similar fashion through four stages in a fixed order. He stated that these stages differ in the quantity of information acquired and the quality of knowledge and understanding as well. Movement from one stage to the next occurs when a child reaches an appropriate level of maturation and is exposed to relevant types of experiences. Without these relevant experiences, children might be incapable of reaching their highest level of cognitive growth. The four stages are known as the sensorimotor, preoperational, concrete operational, and formal operational stages.

What are the four developmental stages in Piaget's theory?

(1) **Sensorimotor Stage: Birth to Two years.** During the initial part of this stage the child has relatively little competence in representing the environment through the use of images, language, or other kind of symbols. Children at the beginning of this stage do not understand the principle of object permanence, that is they are not aware that objects and people exist when they are out of sight. However, at about nine months, the awareness of this principle begins to emerge as children start searching for objects that are hidden.

see major detail:
(1)
(2)
(3)
(4)

(2) **Preoperational Stage: Two to Seven Years.** During this stage the development of language is critical. Children at first create internal systems that allow them to describe people, events, and feelings. Preoperational children are engrossed in egocentric thought, believing that everyone views the world exactly as they do. Preoperational children believe that everyone thinks like they do. If children in this stage cover their eyes so that they cannot see, they believe that others cannot see them, even though they may be in full view. They reason that since they cannot see, no one else can see either.

Children in this stage do not understand the principle of conservation, the knowledge that quantity is unrelated to the arrangement and the visual appearance of objects. They do not understand that amount, volume, or length of an object does not change when its shape or configuration is changed.

wavey lines indicate important definitions

(3) **Concrete Operations Stage: Seven to Twelve Years.** The beginning of this stage is marked by mastery of the principle of conservation. During this stage, children develop the ability to think in a more logical manner, and they begin to overcome some of the egocentric characteristics of the preoperational period. Also, they are able to understand the principle of reversibility, the idea that some changes can be undone by reversing an earlier action. For instance, they understand that a ball of clay may be shaped into a coil and then be reshaped into a ball again.

key terms are in boxes

(4) **Formal Operations Stage: Twelve Years to Adulthood.** This stage is characterized by abstract, formal, and logical thinking. Children in this stage are no longer tied to events that are observed in their environment. Formal operational thought emerges during the teenage years, but in some cases is used only infrequently. In fact, some individuals never reach this stage at all. It is estimated that only about 40–60 percent of college students and 25 percent of the general population reach this level of thinking.

FIGURE 3.3 SAMPLE OF MARKED TEXT

Another method uses the concept of advanced organizers such as the table of contents, chapter headings, and subheadings. By inserting numerals and letters, as in an outline format, you can create an overview of the chapter by labeling the headings in your text. This helps you to gain a clear view of the chapter organization and creates an organizational framework for the information to follow.

You might also choose to write key ideas or questions in the margins to help you remember the important points. Textbooks, like this one, often purposely leave wide margins, like the ones in this text, so students will have space to record their reactions to the material.

The way you decide to mark a textbook section should or will vary according to your purposes and the kind of material you are marking. Try several methods until you find some that are right for you.

Continue to the Next ☐

You are now ready to move forward and read to the next Control ☐, where you will once again test your comprehension. Frequent assessment of your thinking will help you control your effectiveness in reading and remembering. This metacognitive information will assist you later to personalize BICUM to meet your specific needs.

Also, stopping every so often will help you stay focused as you read. Many students find that it is motivating to hold themselves accountable for their comprehension. Recognizing that at every Control ☐ you will have to paraphrase what you have read is a deterrent to getting off-track. BICUM trains you to be responsible for what you read and to consistently search for meaning. In short, you are gaining control over your reading.

Read to End of Study Block

Repeat this pattern of reading from one Control □ to another until you finish the pages you planned to cover or until it is time for your break. Remember the recommended 50:10:50 study ratio (or whatever times you chose for yourself) and spend a few minutes away from your studies. Remember that your mind needs this time to consolidate the information you have been learning. Also, study breaks can refresh you and give you a renewed desire to continue. Be disciplined enough to keep your breaks to around 10 minutes.

No, I Don't Understand

Use Fix-up Strategies

If you cannot paraphrase what you have read, you need to clear up your comprehension problems using methods called "fix-up strategies." At first, try these five strategies in the order they are listed, as each one builds upon the other. Later, after you have tried and observed the effectiveness of each strategy, you may use your metacognitive skills to rearrange, add, or eliminate specific strategies.

1. Reread

Probably the most useful fix-up strategy, if properly used, is rereading. Good readers use this approach naturally when they recognize they are confused. If the problem is difficult material or complex relationships among ideas, then a second reading is helpful. However, if the reason for lack of understanding is daydreaming, then frequent rereading can be a waste of time. Focused concentration

Rereading is often sufficient to clear up comprehension problems.

will help eliminate unnecessary rereading and help you finish assignments in less time.

As you practice the strategies in this study-reading program, you will likely find that rereading is often sufficient to clear up your comprehension problems.

2. Read Ahead

If rereading did not clear up your confusion, try reading ahead. Sometimes, your Control □ might be placed at a point where the author has not finished explaining a concept. Simply reading ahead a short distance may clear up your comprehension problem.

3. Define Unfamiliar Words

The next fix-up strategy is defining unfamiliar words. It is a good idea to use this strategy sparingly because stopping to look up every word in the dictionary as you read can interrupt your train of thought and increase your confusion. You may find that as you continue reading, the author actually defines the words that confuse you.

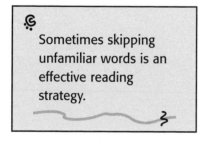

Sometimes skipping unfamiliar words is an effective reading strategy.

Some students are surprised to learn that skipping unfamiliar words is actually an effective reading strategy. Certain words are central to understanding, and others are only marginally important. However, if you are having difficulty with a section because you have skipped words, it is time to see if defining these words increases your understanding.

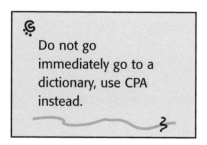

Do not go immediately go to a dictionary, use CPA instead.

Do not immediately go to a dictionary. Remember the acronym CPA that was discussed in Chapter 2, to help you remember to first use the context, the words surrounding the unknown words, to discover their meaning. In many instances the context gives you enough clues to help you decide the meaning. For example, see if you can define the following underlined words by using the rest of the words in the sentences as clues.

Research will probably *corroborate* that fact.

Difficult words may *hinder* your comprehension.

Did you decide that *corroborate* means "to confirm or support"? If you did, you are correct. To *hinder* means "to interfere with" or "stop." Did you figure out that meaning from context?

Sometimes, though, the context does not provide sufficient clues to help you define the words you skipped. If this happens, using familiar word parts may assist you. If using context clues and word parts do not give you enough information to figure out the meaning of an unfamiliar word, then consult an authoritative source. For instance, look the words up in the glossary at the back of your textbook. Glossaries are much easier to use than dictionaries because they define words specifically as they are used in the textbook and because there are fewer words to search through. However, the limited number of entries may mean that the words you want defined are not included.

If this is the case, your next choice is to consult the dictionary. Since some words have multiple meanings, be careful to select definitions that match the way the words are used in the sentences you are considering.

Lastly, and perhaps easiest of all, ask someone what the words mean. Be sure that the person you choose is knowledgeable so he/she can correctly define the words as they are used in your textbook.

Recognize that in practice, you may select any of these methods for defining unfamiliar words. Simply use whichever methods work best for you, depending on the circumstance.

4. Read Out Loud

If the previous three fix-up strategies did not clear up the problem, it is time to employ some less conventional tactics. Follow the next few suggestions if you are in an area where noise and movement would not bother others. Stand up in your study area and stretch several times. Take a few deep breaths, then pick up your textbook. Begin to pace, reading sentence by sentence out loud.

The change in position and the movement, combined with the power of hearing your own voice, make this strategy especially effective. Be cautioned, however, that the amount of material you read out loud should be limited. Many students are so successful reading out loud that they erroneously decide to read all their assignments vocally. This is not a wise choice. Reading out loud is much too time consuming. College courses require a tremendous amount of reading. It is much better to train yourself to read silently and to save vocal reading as a fix-up strategy.

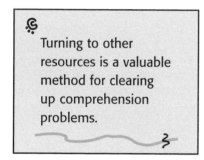

Changing position and occasionally hearing your own voice can be a very effective reading strategy.

5. Mark with "?" to Clear up Later

The final fix-up strategy is marking the text with a "?" to clear up later. Do not make the mistake of thinking this is an admission of failure. Turning to other resources for assistance is a valuable method for clearing up comprehension problems. Simply place a "?" beside the section that you find confusing. Then continue reading the remainder of your assignment.

Turning to other resources is a valuable method for clearing up comprehension problems.

Later, try one or more of the following methods to clear up the chapter parts you marked. For example, you might contact a fellow student who is doing well in the class and ask for assistance. Perhaps locating a less difficult textbook on the subject would also be helpful. Reading from that book might give you enough additional background knowledge to help you understand the more challenging version of the material given in your text. Certainly asking your instructor for assistance would be a good option. Teachers are usually impressed with students who care enough to read assignments and ask for clarification on specific areas of concern.

Identify Patterns of Organization

Authors understand the importance of the arrangement of ideas in aiding our memory, so they purposely structure the textbook chapter in ways that will help the students see the relationships among the ideas. Although there are many other patterns of organization, Appendix B discusses only a few of the most common: listing, sequence, comparison and contrast, cause and effect, and illustration. See this appendix for a chart listing the basic-elements of these patterns and a brief discussion of each one.

By becoming aware of the way authors arrange details to support their main points, readers can gain additional insights into the information being discussed. As students become aware of clue words that signal the pattern being used, it helps them to anticipate and follow the author's train of thought. When the organization is clear, it enhances memory as well as comprehension.

Students often ask, "Do I have to identify topics, main ideas, supporting details and patterns for every paragraph I read?" The answer is "no." This would be much too time consuming. However, with repeated practice of these skills, you will begin to identify, or "pull out," this crucial information naturally and become a more effective reader. Using the strategies already explained in the *Ready* stage and reading actively, as explained in the section that follows, will also help increase your ability to automatically locate important information. Eventually, you will probably only need to consciously identify topics, main ideas, and major details when you are faced with especially difficult material or when preparing for challenging exams.

Becoming proficient in determining key information requires practice and application. By raising your level of awareness of these important skills and regularly searching for meaning as you read, these powerful processes will become a natural part of reading for understanding and retention. A helpful analogy might be to think about how

> Becoming proficient in determining key information requires practice and application.

slow and difficult the process feels for someone first learning to type. Once proficiency is reached, what once took conscious effort soon becomes automatic. Remember that your task in the *Read* stage is to understand the textbook chapter. It is frustrating, if not impossible, to remember confusing material. After you have completed the first two stages in BICUM, *Ready* and *Read,* you should be able to confidently say, "I understand what I have read."

When you can do this, you are ready to move to stage three, *Reduce*. Here you will select the important information you need for testing purposes and reproduce that information in a condensed or reduced form.

Summary

Reading college textbooks can be tough because it requires skills not often taught in high school. Actively searching for meaning and training your mind not to wander are keys to success. The sentence "Reading is reading only when meaning is coming through" is especially applicable when reading textbooks. All information in textbooks is not of equal value. Identifying topics, main ideas, and major supporting details will help you locate and understand the most important information.

Being active when you read includes talking with textbook authors, visualizing, predicting, finding answers to questions, pacing yourself with a pencil, and clustering. When you come to Control □'s, pause and test your understanding. If you can paraphrase what you have read, mark and highlight the text and predict possible test questions; then move to the next section. If you cannot paraphrase your reading, use one or more of the five fix-up strategies to get back on track. When you have successfully completed stage one and two, *Ready* and *Read*, you should then proceed to stage three, *Reduce*.

Review Questions

1. What questions should you ask in order to identify the topic of a paragraph? What are some benefits of learning to make topics precise?

2. What questions should you ask in order to determine main ideas? Why are main ideas so important?

3. Discuss ways to formulate the main idea of a paragraph when the main idea is unstated.

4. What purposes do major supporting details serve in paragraphs? Why is it important to be able to distinguish between major and minor details?

5. How can you read actively? Give at least two active reading techniques you plan to use in your studies.

6. What are some benefits for learning to use paraphrasing effectively?

7. How do you presently mark and highlight your text? What could you change in the future to make your text marking more effective?

8. What are five fix-up strategies you can use if you do not understand what you are reading? Which ones do you feel might help you the most?

9. What options for defining unknown words are given in this chapter? Which of these options do you use most often? Why?

10. Once you have marked a confusing section of text with a "?", what are some ways to clear up your comprehension problem?

Metacognitive Insights

There are many strategies in the *Read* stage. Which ones work best for you? Completing the following sentences will help you begin to decide. On the remaining lines add additional information that you have learned about yourself after reading the chapter and completing the activities.

1. Identifying the topic of a paragraph is _____
_____
_____

2. Determining main ideas is _____
_____
_____

3. The best way for me to be active when I read is _____
_____
_____

4. When I stop at Control □'s, I _____
_____
_____

5. Reading out loud for me is _____
_____
_____

ADDITIONAL INSIGHTS

_____
_____
_____
_____
_____

*R*educe

- Post View

- Answer Questions

- Organize for Recall

(Select 1)

– make outlines

– take notes

– write summaries

– create maps

REDUCING THE AMOUNT TO LEARN

We are feeling the full force of a knowledge explosion of unbelievable magnitude . . . Knowledge is doubling every twenty months."
—JAMES I. BROWN
READING POWER, 4TH ed.

Keeping pace with the knowledge explosion sounds like an impossible task. Fortunately, you do not have to move at the same speed that knowledge is advancing in order to be educated. But you will need to learn information specific to a chosen major. Furthermore, since knowledge continues to increase rapidly it is essential that you "learn how to learn." Then you can be aware of the new developments in your field and continue to learn long after you have completed your college degree.

Throughout college, you will likely be assigned thousands of pages to read. It is not necessary for you to memorize all these pages of required reading. Even the most demanding of professors does not expect you to remember every bit of information. Instead, use what you learned in the last chapter to single out pertinent information, ideas, or concepts. You learned to identify topics, main ideas, and major supporting details. Hold on to this information, and let the other information go.

Forgetting unimportant information is actually a useful "house cleaning" practice for your mind. Forgetting makes way for crucial information and helps ensure that it does not get lost at the expense of useless data. In this chapter, you will learn how to reduce and organize essential information.

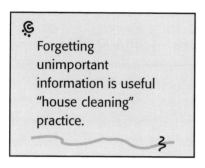

Forgetting unimportant information is useful "house cleaning" practice.

Many students think that when they have finished reading their assignments, they have completed their homework. Often, this is not enough. If you need to remember material for an extended time, you will need to use some of the strategies in the last two stages in BICUM: *Reduce* and *Retain*. This chapter will cover *Reduce* strategies. Chapter 5 will cover *Retain*.

Reducing important chapter information can save you time when you study for tests. Memorizing information in a reduced form can make learning complex material more manageable, especially over multiple chapters. *Rereading textbooks is one of the most commonly used test preparation methods, but also one of the most inefficient.* Creating reduced forms of chapters as you read, then using those forms as study guides is a wiser and more efficient use of your time.

Recognize too that you do not have to reduce everything you read. As with all of the stages and strategies in BICUM, reducing is an option to use when it fits your needs. Learn the strategies well, and practice them carefully. Then, use your metacognitive awareness to decide if you need to reduce material and which strategies you should follow. Experiment with the following techniques to learn how to select, organize, and reduce textbook material.

Post-View

You learned in chapter 2 about the benefits of previewing before beginning to read assignments. This strategy helped you see the overall organization of textbook chapters and the relationships of the various sections within them. You learned, too, that previewing contributes to using advanced organizers, which prepare your mind for the upcoming information in the chapter. Remember that advance organizing leads to understanding, which is usually a prerequisite for learning and remembering.

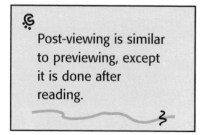

Post-viewing is similar to previewing, except it is done after reading.

Post-viewing is a simple strategy that is similar to previewing. The main difference is that it is done after you read, instead of before. In order for post-viewing to be effective it should be done as soon after the reading as possible, but at least within twenty-four hours.

To post-view, begin as you did when you previewed. Look over the chapter, noticing the overall structure. Now, check to see if you understand the various sections and how they fit into the chapter as a whole. If you were successful in reading for meaning, the post-view should be an enjoyable experience as you review the information you have learned. However, if you notice parts of the chapter that are still unclear, you may need to pause and take a few minutes to clear up the confusion. This is accomplished by using one or more of the fix-up strategies listed in the *Read* stage. (See pp. 95–98.)

Taking time to correct comprehension problems when they arise may prevent more serious problems later, when you are studying for a test. Remembering information that is confusing is a very difficult task. The post-view is another metacognitive technique that helps you recognize and correct comprehension problems.

Do not take a great deal of time post-viewing. Unless you find areas of confusion, about five minutes is usually sufficient. Like previews, quick post-views can be very effective.

Answer Questions

Once you are familiar with the structure of the chapter and the information in it, check to see if you found the answers to the questions you either selected or created in the *Ready* stage (see p. 48). If you marked them during the *Read* stage (see p. 63), it should be an easy process to find the answers now. Be careful not to skip any of the questions. Remember that many teachers consider the answers to chapter questions the most important information in textbooks. If your instructor feels this way, be certain to locate all this information.

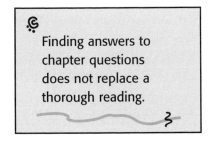

Finding answers to chapter questions does not replace a thorough reading.

Because answers to chapter questions are often a primary source of test material, some students are tempted to search for them without reading the chapter. Resist this temptation. Recognize that finding these pieces of information will not replace thorough knowledge gained by reading the chapter. Identifying information in isolation from the surrounding discussion is often confusing, and it is difficult to see clearly the relationships among the ideas. You will find it easier to remember information if you can see the bigger picture, which reading the chapter provides. Since most college professors expect a deeper understanding of the chapter concepts, just copying down answers to questions will not give you the information you need to be successful.

Organize for Recall

Memorizing an entire textbook is not an impossible task, since your mind can store billions of pieces of information. In fact, the two-pound human brain can store more data than today's advanced computers. However, for most people memorizing hundreds of pages would take far too much time. It is much better to organize essential information in a simplified or reduced form and not spend countless hours trying to memorize everything. You can then use the valuable time you save for other important aspects of your life. Two ways to improve memory are to organize and cluster related information.

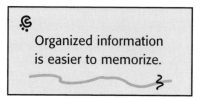

Organized information
is easier to memorize.

Did you know that organized information is easier to memorize than unorganized information? Kenneth Higbee (1993), a renowned memory expert, uses the following example to illustrate the point. Give yourself one minute to memorize the number below.

912161923263033

Now cover up the number and write it on a piece of paper. Were you able to recall it? If you did, congratulations! Could you write it an hour, a day, or a month from now? Not likely. Most students could not repeat the number unless they had another chance to relearn it. A simple change in organization, though, could make this number easy to memorize and even retain over a long period of time. Here is the same number, this time clustered in a specific manner.

9 12 16 19 23 26 30 33

Do you see how the number is organized? Is there a pattern? Give yourself a minute to see how separating this number can help you understand and remember it more easily. Do you recognize the relationships between the segments? Did you try adding specific numbers to each segment to discover the pattern?

You probably discovered that the pattern is to alternate adding 3 and 4 to the numerical unit. Notice that when you add 3 to 9, you get 12; when you add 4 to 12, you get 16; when you add 3 to 16, you get 19, and so on. Now that the number is organized, could you easily reproduce it in an hour from now, a week, or a month? Of course you could; the organization and knowing the key to it makes all the difference.

Using organizing as an aid to memory works not only with numbers but also with written text. It is well worth your time to organize material before you attempt to learn it. You will find that organized material is not only easier to memorize but is also more readily retrieved, and it stays in your memory longer.

Reduction Techniques

Once you have marked and highlighted the important ideas during the *Read* stage, you are ready to reduce this information into a simplified version on separate paper. You do this by cutting out nonessential ideas.

The pages that follow will explain and model for you a number of reduction methods, each of which has different benefits. Since students learn in different ways, the selections you choose will likely influence how easily you learn information. You should learn several of the methods, since some ways lend themselves to certain material better than others. As you continue your college courses, you will appreciate having an assortment of reduction techniques from which to choose. Also, you will probably find that you clearly prefer some methods over others. Recognizing your natural preferences is part of metacognitive awareness. Consciously notice which techniques work best for you.

In this chapter you will learn four of the most popular and effective reduction methods for organizing textbook material. These methods are (1) making outlines, (2) taking notes, (3) writing summaries, and (4) creating maps. Keep in mind that no matter which method you choose, you should make your reduced form complete enough so that you can study for tests directly from it. That is, for the most part, you should not have to go back to your textbook to find additional information to prepare successfully for tests.

Refer to Figure 4.1 for a sample article that will be reduced with these four methods. As you read the selection titled "The Roots of American Government," try to predict which of the ideas are the most important and would likely be included in a reduced form. Later, when you examine the sample outline, notes, summary, and map of this article, notice whether your predictions were accurate. Also be aware that there are other ways to reduce this information; these are only samples. Different instructors stress different aspects of a subject, and discovering what they may emphasize is part of the learning process.

Make Outlines

Outlining is a formal method for organizing information, although most students use informal outlines as a study method. Outlining includes labeling ideas, identifying their levels of importance, and showing the relationships among ideas. Outlines allow you to readily see how the key ideas relate to one another and how effectively authors back up their main points. Textbook chapters typically lend themselves to outlining because headings and subheadings are commonly included. These serve as useful organizational cues for arranging outlines.

> Textbooks are often easy to outline because they have headings and subheadings.

Outlines utilize Roman numerals, letters, numbers, and indentations to display information. You probably learned the basics of outlining in one of your high school classes. Perhaps your teacher introduced you to a formal outline form, in which you had to use the proper order of enumeration and lettering. When outlining a textbook chapter, however, you do not have to follow formal rules. Instead, record the ideas as you see them, and do not worry about formal formatting. It is more important that your outline be clear to you than that it adhere to strict rules. Just be sure to include the important information and to accurately show the relationships that the author described. Figure 4.2 is a sample outline of the article on "The Roots of American Government."

The Roots of American Government

As America began to emerge as a nation, its predominantly English population looked to their former homeland as a model of limited government. While other eighteenth century European nations acknowledged the divine right of their kings to have almost unlimited control over their lives, England did not give their leaders this power. British courts operated on a system known as **common law.** This form of government guaranteed trial by jury and protection of life, liberty, and property. These fundamental rights were usually defended by the courts and were generally respected by the king and the English Parliament.

British law was greatly influenced by the English philosopher John Locke (1632–1704) who proclaimed that government must be restrained in its powers if it is to serve the common good of the people. The roots of Locke's theories came from the Greeks and Romans and stressed individual rights and the limited role of government. Locke's writings were widely read and became an inspiration to a generation of American leaders. For example, one of Locke's books, *Two Treatises of Government* (1689), strongly influenced Thomas Jefferson, the major author of the Declaration of Independence. Jefferson declared Locke to be among the greatest men of all time.

One of the major principles advanced by Locke was that people have **inalienable rights** or natural rights, including those of life, liberty, and property. These rights, Locke believed, belonged to people in their natural state, even before governments were created. He said that people came together and entered into a **social contract** for the protection afforded them by organized government. Locke declared that the justification for government's existence was found in its ability to protect human rights better than individuals could protect themselves. He said further that these governments could not morally take away people's rights, nor were people obligated to surrender them to their leaders. Locke also believed that when governments did not adequately protect inalienable rights, people had the right, even the duty, to rebel against their governments. He firmly stated that all people should have the right to decide who governs them.

John Locke's ideas were part of a larger philosophical movement called the **Enlightenment.** This movement, in eighteenth-century Europe, sought to understand the proper order of nature and society. Locke's ideas dominated the Enlightenment theories of government to the same degree that Sir Isaac Newton's ideas dominated Enlightenment theories of science. Locke's theories on government had special appeal for the American colonists who among all people at this time had the most free government and personal freedoms. Locke's revolutionary ideas about rulers and natural rights provided the roots that were needed to form a limited government to preserve those freedoms and lay a foundation for the new American government.

Adapted from *The American Democracy*
by Thomas E. Patterson

FIGURE 4.1 THE ROOTS OF AMERICAN GOVERNMENT

Do you see the relationships among the ideas in the preceding sample? You can create these connections by using the information contained in the main ideas and the major supporting details, in which authors introduce general points and then go into detail explaining them. The more general ideas should stand out in the left margin, while more specific information about the topic should be indented. This shows levels of importance and their relationships. Is the organization of the previous outline clear and understandable to you?

The outline in Figure 4.2 is somewhat artificial because normally it is unnecessary to create an outline that extensive for just one page. When you are outlining an entire chapter, the author helps you to see some of the main points and their relationships. This will become more evident as you go through the following steps.

How to Make a Successful Outline

Preparing the text:

- Locate the largest bold headings in the chapter. These are usually the most general topics. Notice that many textbooks place the general headings near the left margin and indent the more specific subheadings slightly toward the right. If headings are in the same font and print size they are usually of equal importance. Label them in your text with Roman numerals: I, II, III, IV, etc.

- Check for subheadings (the next size of bold print). Label each of these topics in your text with a capital letter: A, B, C, D.

- Check for smaller subheadings; then label them numerically: 1, 2, 3, 4.

Creating the outline:

- Begin your outline on paper by recording the title of the chapter.

- Record the heading you labeled with Roman numeral I.

The Roots of American Government

I. America looked to England as a model of limited government.
   A. British courts operated on "common law."
      1. Guaranteed trial by jury
      2. Protected life, liberty & property
   B. Fundamental rights guarded by courts
II. British law was influenced by John Locke.
   A. His ideas had Greek & Roman roots.
      1. Stressed individual rights
      2. Endorsed limited role of government
   B. Locke's writings influenced American leaders such as Thomas Jefferson.
III. A major principle of Locke's was a belief in inalienable rights.
   A. Natural rights existing before govt.
   B. Rights to life, liberty & property
   C. People come together in "social contracts" to protect rights.
      1. Govt. protect better than individuals
      2. Govt. can't morally take rights away
      3. Duty of people to rebel if governments don't protect rights
      4. People can choose who governs them
IV. Locke's ideas were part of the Enlightenment.
   A. An 18th century philosophical movement to understand nature & society
   B. Locke's ideas dominated government theories of Enlightenment.
      1. Theories appealed to American colonists
      2. His ideas used to form America's limited govt. to protect natural rights

FIGURE 4.2 SAMPLE OUTLINE

- Leave space after each heading to add supporting details. Indent and add the information that you found under that heading and labeled A, B, C, D, etc.

- If you found specific subheadings labeled numerically 1, 2, 3, 4, indent and record them under the more general topic they support.

Figure 4.3 shows the basic outline form using Roman numerals, letters, numbers, and indentations.

You can construct outlines with either complete sentences or short phrases. Either choice is fine; experiment with what works for you. Your outline should allow you to see at a glance the most important points and their supports. As a result, you will probably notice that memorizing information from your outline is much easier than trying to learn material directly from a textbook.

Benefits of Outlines

If you appreciate order and do not mind following a few simple rules, outlining may be the reduction form you prefer. Many students report that outlines make helpful study guides because the formal arrangement of information helps them see the overall organization of

TITLE

I. **First Main Point**
   A. **Major Supporting Detail**
   B. **Major Supporting Detail**
      1. **Minor Supporting Detail**
      2. **Minor Supporting Detail**
   C. **Major Supporting Detail**
II. **Second Main Point**
   A. **Major Supporting Detail**
      1. **Minor Supporting Detail**
      2. **Minor Supporting Detail**
   B. **Major Supporting Detail**

FIGURE 4.3 FORMAT FOR OUTLINES

METACOGNITIVE TRAINING ACTIVITY
Making Outlines
·℣· MTA 4.1 ·℣·

⅗ DIRECTIONS:
You will create and assess the reduction technique of outlining a
   textbook chapter.
Choose to outline a chapter that you will be tested on in one of your
   classes.
Use the guidelines and the samples discussed in this chapter to aid
   you.

1. Record the title of the course, textbook, and chapter.

2. Outline the chapter. Remember that your finished outline
   should include all of the information you will need to prepare
   for a test on the material. Hand in a copy of the outline with
   this MTA.

3. What features of outlining are most helpful? Why?

4. What parts of outlining challenge you the most? Explain.

5. Self Grade _____% and brief justification.

entire chapters. Outlining is especially useful if the
information to learn is long and complex.

Take Notes

Taking notes is another method of reducing textbook
material. Many students prefer this informal approach of
writing brief phrases that cover important information. As
with the other reduction forms you have learned, there are a
variety of systems for taking notes. However, some fifty
years ago Dr. Walter Pauk from Cornell University created a
system of note taking that is distinctive in its effectiveness.
Named after the university, **Cornell Notes** have been used
successfully by students ever since. This system is simple
and can have far reaching benefits. Its unique format,
shown in Figure 4.4, has a major right-hand section for

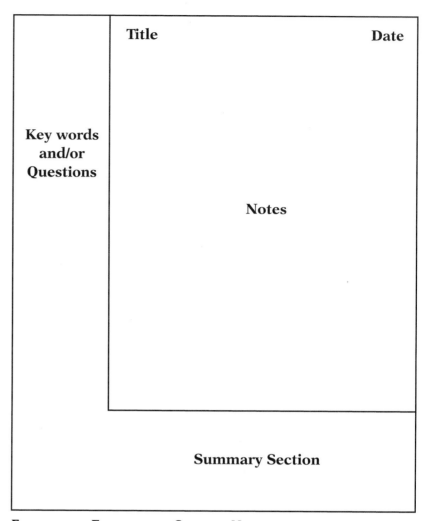

FIGURE 4.4 FORMAT FOR CORNELL NOTES

notes, a left-hand column for key words and/or questions, and a section for summaries at the bottom of the page.

Figure 4.5 shows a page of Cornell Notes on "The Roots of American Government." Study the example. Can you see how its distinctive arrangement on the pages gives added benefits to note taking?

How to Take Successful Cornell Notes

Refer to the following steps for specific suggestions for using the reduction process.

- Create the Cornell Notes format by dividing the paper into three sections. Draw a vertical line about

Roots of Amer. Govt.   11-26-96

Amer. govt. model	Amer. saw Eng. as limited govt. model
	— British courts used "common law"
"common law"	• guaranteed jury trial
	• protected life, liberty, property
source & influence of Locke's ideas	— John Locke's ideas, with Greek & Roman roots influenced Eng. law
	• stressed indiv. rights
	• endorsed limited govt.
	— Locke's writings influenced Amer. leaders, eg. Thomas Jefferson
What are "inalien-able rights?"	Belief in "inalienable rights," a major principle of Locke's
	• natural rights existed before govt.
	• right to life, liberty, property
What is a "social contract?"	— "Social contracts" provide protection
	• govts. protect better than indiv.
	• govts. can't morally remove rights
	• duty to rebel against bad govt.
	• right to choose who governed by
How did Locke's ideas impact Amer. govt?	Locke's ideas dominated 18th century Enligtenment theories of govt.
	— Revolutionary ideas appealed to American colonists
	— Americans used his ideas to form govt. with limited powers

This page discusses a model for limited govt., "common law," "inalienable rights," responsibilities of govt., & how John Locke's ideas influenced Amer. govt..

FIGURE 4.5 SAMPLE CORNELL NOTES

2½ inches from the left side of a sheet of notebook paper to create two major sections. The large section on the right is for notes. The narrow section on the left is a "cue column" for study and review. Draw another line 2½ inches from the bottom of the paper to create the summary section.

- Title and date your notes.

- The section on the right is the only section that is to be completed while in class or reading your assignment. In the note-taking section use your usual method of note taking or follow the general note-taking tips given on the next page.

- Review your notes in the right hand section as soon as possible. To increase retention it is important to do this within twenty-four hours of taking the notes. The cue column on the left provides an excellent opportunity to predict possible test questions. Do this by processing the material and placing questions and key words in the cue column. Write relevant questions, new vocabulary words, or other cues that help you to condense the information. These cues will be useful for future study and review.

- In the bottom section, write a one- or two-sentence summary of the information on each page of notes, or summarize all of the main points in a paragraph at the bottom of the last page.

- To study for a test, cover the wide section of notes on the right. Read the key words or questions in the narrow cue column. Use them to test yourself on the information in the notes section.

- If you remembered the information correctly, move to the next key word or question. If you did not, uncover the right column and review your notes. Then cover the right side again and try to recall your notes. Repeat this process to learn all of the information.

Cornell Notes are excellent in helping you process material at a deeper level. They help you to learn the information to the recall level, not just to the recognition level. For many students their method of study is to leaf through information that they have read and say to themselves, "I know that" or "I remember that." Because they recognize material that they have seen before, they falsely assume that they know it well enough to reproduce it on a test or use it later. Actually, they have only begun to learn the information.

On the other hand, when students take Cornell Notes and use them properly, they force themselves to process information at a deeper recall level. By using the review column to test themselves on their notes they have to pull the information instead of seeing it front of them.

General Note-Taking Tips

There are several ways you can take notes in addition to the Cornell style. The following general tips apply not only to Cornell Notes but also to any other style. Some students prefer to write complete sentences, others use phrases, and still others combine the two. Since note taking is informal, it does not matter which of these you choose. What is important is to include all the key information.

Be sure to organize your notes to show relationships. Start new ideas at the margins; then indent to show subordinate ideas. Also, be sure to leave space between different concepts so that thoughts do not blend together and become confusing. Write legibly so that you will be able to understand your notes later.

Personalize your notes by creating abbreviations and symbols that save you time. If you practice using these when writing notes from your textbooks, you can improve your efficiency so that taking notes during lectures is also easier.

SUGGESTIONS FOR USING SYMBOLS AND ABBREVIATIONS
Experiment with the following 10 suggestions for using symbols and abbreviations:

1. Use symbols instead of phrases.

$\rightarrow$	Leads to
$\neq$	Does not equal
$\underline{f}$	Frequency

2. Leave out the periods in standard abbreviations.

Mt	mountain
Dept	department

3. Use only the first syllable of frequently used terms.

Pol	politics
Dem	democracy

4. Eliminate the final letters. Use just enough of the beginning of a word to form an easily recognizable abbreviation.

assoc	associate
biol	biological

5. Omit vowels from the middle of words, and retain only enough consonants to provide a recognizable skeleton of the word.

gvt	government
estmt	estimate

6. Use an apostrophe in place of letters.

am't	amount
cont'd	continued

7. Use "g" to represent *ing* endings.

ckg	checking
decrg	decreasing

8. Leave out the words "a" and "the."

9. Use symbols for commonly recurring connective words.

w/o	without
vs	versus

10. Spell out short words such as *in, at, to, but, for* and *key*. Using symbols or abbreviations for these words, which often clarify the relationships between ideas, will make your notes confusing.

The previous suggestions are commonly used in taking notes, but you should create your own system. Make sure that if you develop your own symbols and abbreviations, create a key in your text or chapter so that you will remember how you used them.

Benefits of Taking Notes

Because taking notes can be done in many informal ways, it is perhaps the most common textbook reduction form. Recording information without concern for rigid structure can be both clarifying and energizing. To effectively transfer information from the text to your notes requires that you process what you are reading and are actively involved in your learning. As mentioned earlier, taking notes from textbooks where you can organize your thoughts and write at your own pace can also help prepare you for taking lecture notes, which must usually be recorded at a faster pace.

METACOGNITIVE TRAINING ACTIVITY
Taking Notes
·꒳· MTA 4.2 ·꒳·

≩ DIRECTIONS:
Take Cornell notes on a textbook chapter that you will be tested on in one of your classes.
Your notes should contain all of the information you will need to prepare for a test on the material.

1. Record the name of the course, text, and chapter.

2. Take Cornell Notes using the guidelines discussed in this chapter.

3. What is the purpose of the narrow column on the left side of the paper?

4. What do you consider the advantages of taking Cornell Notes versus other note-taking systems?

5. What is one area of your Cornell Notes that needs to be improved? Explain.

6. Will you use this system of note-taking again? Why or why not?

7. Self Grade _____% and brief justification.

Write Summaries

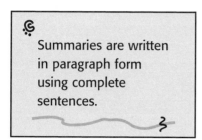

Summaries are written in paragraph form using complete sentences.

Summaries are brief versions of textbook chapters that include only the most important ideas in paragraph form. Unlike outlines, maps, or note reductions, summaries must be written in complete sentences. Because summaries should be paraphrased or written in your own words yet maintain the author's meaning, these study aids can be challenging to create. Simply copying sentences from the text does not ensure understanding. Also, copying sentences directly from textbooks encourages **plagiarism,** which is using another person's words or ideas and not giving the author credit for them. If you develop skill in paraphrasing, you will likely not be tempted to plagiarize.

Writing summaries demands that you view information in a broad context and requires that you see the overall importance of ideas and the relationships among them. If part of a textbook chapter is confusing to you, summarizing it will be difficult, if not impossible. Your ease in creating a summary will test how clearly you understood what you read. Figure 4.6 is a student summary of "The Roots of American Government."

After reading the sample summary, were you able to see that the key points had been paraphrased or rewritten in an abbreviated form? Compare the sample summary to the following guidelines to help you better understand how to write summaries of your own.

How to Write a Successful Summary

- Begin with a title to remind yourself of the subject being discussed.

- Paraphrase the first main idea of the passage as the beginning sentence of the summary.

- Follow the order and sequence the author used.

- Include the main points the author included.

- Add major supporting details only as needed to clarify main ideas.

The Roots of American Government

As America began as a nation, it looked to England as a model of limited government. Englishmen's rights were protected by a system called "common law," and British law was greatly influenced by the philosopher John Locke. His philosophies had Greek and Roman roots which stressed the limited role of government and individual rights. Locke's theories also greatly influenced Thomas Jefferson, the major author of the Declaration of Independence.

John Locke taught the principle of inalienable or natural rights. He believed that people came together in "social contracts" or formed governments to protect these rights. Locke also believed that people did not have to surrender rights to government, and they should rebel against governments who failed to protect their rights. His revolutionary ideas about rulers and natural rights provided the roots of American government.

FIGURE 4.6 SAMPLE SUMMARY

- Avoid repeating unnecessary words.

- Rewrite the facts and ideas in your own words. Leave out unimportant words and emphasize important ones. Show connections among the important ideas.

- Use connecting words such as *first, second, because,* or *although* to show how your summary fits together and the proper relationship of the sentences to each other. Transition words also help your ideas flow smoothly.

- Obviously, your version needs to be shorter than the original. For study purposes a summary is often about one-fifth to one-fourth the length of the original text.

- Be sure to include all the important information so you can use this summary to prepare for tests.

Benefits of Summaries

Many students find that creating summaries is a great help in mastering textbook information. Even though making summaries can be time-consuming, you will likely find that they are well worth the effort. When exam time arrives, you will be glad you have summaries to study from. It is much easier to learn a shortened version of a chapter than to try to memorize all of it. Summarizing material is especially helpful when preparing for essay tests and when seeing "the big picture" is essential, as in psychology or history classes. As with the other three BICUM reduction forms, summaries should be created after you have read, marked and highlighted the textbook material.

Notice the summaries at the end of each of the chapters in this book. These are brief reductions of the main points of the chapters. Like most summaries in textbooks, though, these do not include all the supporting details. Textbook summaries are included to give you an overview of the chapters and are useful for both previewing and post-viewing but are not complete enough to use as a main source for test preparation. The summaries you create should be more comprehensive and should include all the important information necessary to review in preparation for tests.

METACOGNITIVE TRAINING ACTIVITIES
Writing Summaries
·₹· MTA 4.3 ·₹·

⌇ DIRECTIONS:
Summarize a textbook chapter that you will be tested on in one of
    your classes.
Follow the guidelines discussed in this chapter.

1. Record the course, text, and title of the chapter.

2. Summarize the textbook chapter.

3. Explain the difficulties you experienced in creating a summary.

4. Discuss what you liked about this technique.

5. Self Grade _____% and brief justification.

Create Maps

Mapping is an innovative method of reducing textbook information; this method displays relationships in a visual format. Main ideas and major supporting details are grouped together visually to show how they are related. Maps are a combination of words and pictures that represents concepts and clusters ideas that belong together. Maps represent both the organization of authors' ideas and, perhaps more importantly, students' unique characteristics: their schema, their learning styles, and their creativity. Artistic talent is not necessary to create excellent maps. Stick figures and simple drawings can be very effective. Two crucial ingredients for successful mapping are a willingness to experiment with visual representation of ideas and a desire to accurately portray textbook information.

Figure 4.7 (p. 126) shows some popular styles of maps. The kind of map you choose should fit the type of material you are mapping. For example, a *time line* or *continuum* works well for learning important dates and events in history or steps in an ongoing process as in computer science. A *cycle* is useful for mapping biology concepts such as the life cycle of living things. Because a chapter usually

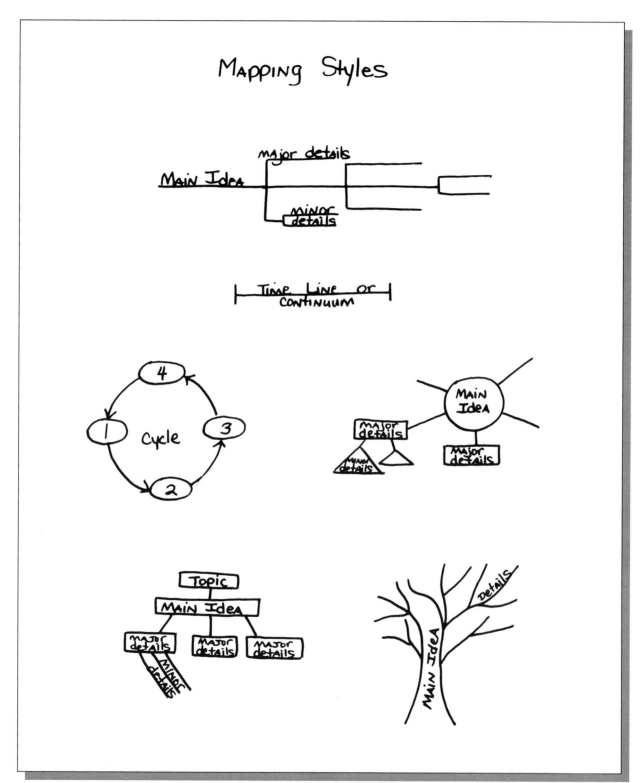

FIGURE 4.7 STYLES OF MAPS

contains a number of main ideas, mapping its information would likely require a variety of ways to connect topics or main points to their major supporting details. Experiment with different styles to identify the ones most useful to you.

Figure 4.8 (p. 128) shows two maps created by two groups of college students on the same article, entitled "The Human Memory Process." Notice that the first map conveys the ideas mostly with pictures, while the second one supplements the pictures with written-in main ideas and key phrases that explain the major supporting details. You will probably agree that neither of these maps displays outstanding artistic ability. Most pictures or drawings in maps will be very simple. Otherwise they would be too difficult and time-consuming to create.

In contrast, the map in Figure 4.9 (p. 129) reveals a great deal of artistic ability. It is important to keep in mind that this map is no more effective than the first two; it just looks more impressive. The artistic quality of a map has little to do with how easily the information is remembered. However, this map portrays in a creative and visual way *how* to create maps and *why* using them is a helpful learning strategy. When you look at this map, you may not understand what every picture represents because the drawings in each map hold more meaning for its creator. When creating a map it is important that the symbols and icons represent the key information for you.

Figure 4.10 (p. 130) is a student map of the article on "The Roots of American Government." Notice the organization and the small icons that represent many of the ideas. Recall that earlier in this chapter, this article was also reduced using outlining, Cornell Notetaking, and summarizing.

How to Create a Successful Map

Even more than the other techniques described in BICUM, mapping requires a keen understanding of the chapter material. You must clearly grasp not only the main ideas and major supporting details but also the relationships among them. The instructions for creating concept maps will not be given in a step-by-step process because maps are

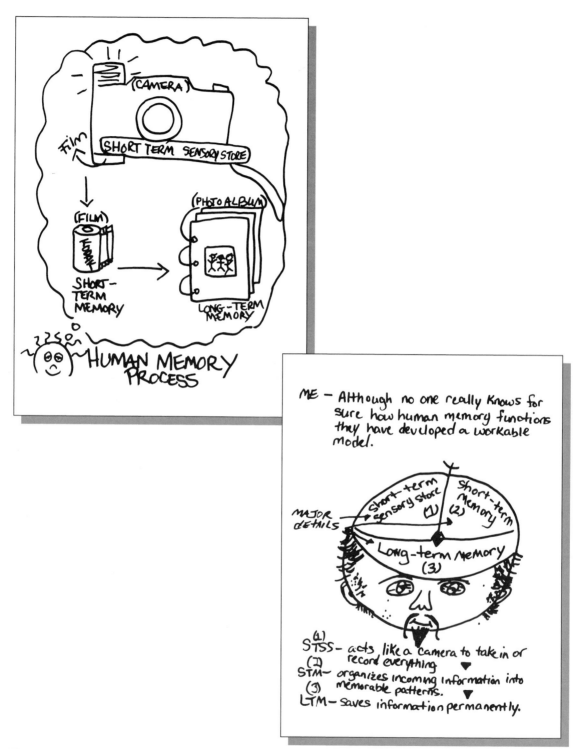

FIGURE 4.8 GROUP MAPS ON HUMAN MEMORY PROCESS

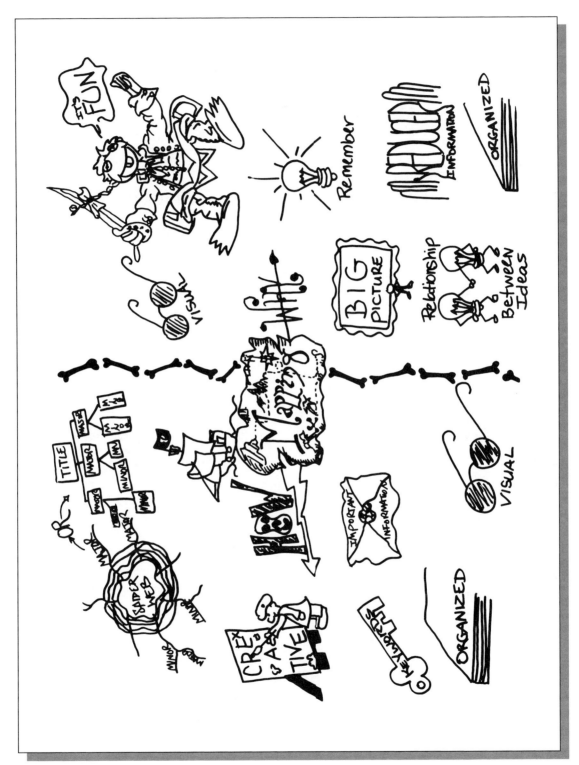

FIGURE 4.9 ARTISTIC MAP OF HOW AND WHY TO USE MAPPING

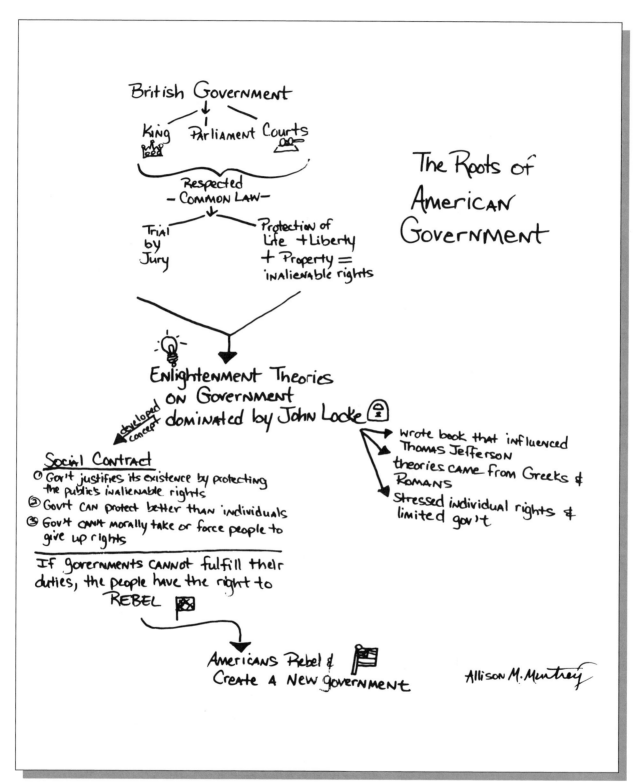

FIGURE 4.10 STUDENT MAP ON "The Roots of American Government"

less structured than outlines, which have a set format to follow.

Mapping can be done in many different ways as long as the important information is shown in a way that illustrates the logical connection between ideas and aids in retention. The absence of clear organization, including too much information, or leaving out key ideas makes a map less effective. Also, a common suggestion made by students for improving a map is to include more visuals instead of too many words. The following guidelines should be helpful as you map information.

- Use unlined paper, preferably larger than notebook size, such as 8½ × 14 or 11 × 14. (Two pieces of paper laid side by side will work well if larger paper is not available.)

- Select a style or method to organize this information that makes sense to you. Keep in mind that you need to accurately portray how ideas fit together and how they relate to the whole.

- Record the chapter title in an obvious place.

- Place chapter headings and subheadings to create an organizational framework.

- Leave plenty of white space between these ideas so that you can make divisions and relationships clear and so that you can add other information.

- Add main ideas and major supporting details.

- Add minor details only if you need to know them.

- Group ideas together that are closely related to show their proper relationships. For example, put major details with the main ideas they support.

- Record ideas in key words and phrases, rather than in complete sentences.

- Use larger print for more important and/or more general information. Use smaller print and indentations to indicate supporting ideas.

- Try using boxes, circles, and other geometric shapes to add clarity.

- Try using different colors for each major section of the map. When recalling information, the color can serve as a memory cue for each cluster of ideas.

- Create large pictures to represent general concepts and small pictures, called **icons,** to represent specific information.

- Check your map for accuracy.

Remember that the primary purpose of mapping is to serve as a memory aid. Maps accomplish this by using visuals that are organized to show clear relationships. The pictures used in mapping are often more easily remembered than are the words. However, for maximum benefit, it is best to include both words and visuals. Combining the two is much more effective than using either of them alone.

METACOGNITIVE TRAINING ACTIVITY
Creating Maps
·ɀ· MTA 4.4 ·ɀ·

⅔ DIRECTIONS:
Create a map from a textbook chapter that you will be tested on in one of your classes.
Follow the guidelines discussed and incorporate the suggestions given.

---

1. Record your course, text, and title of the chapter.

2. Create a map representing the information you will need to know for the test. Hand it in with this MTA.

3. Learn your map to the recall level. One way to do this is to reproduce the map on a blank sheet of paper, without looking at the original.

4. Take the test.

5. What went well?

6. What would you change?

7. Self Grade _____% and brief justification.

If mapping an entire chapter seems overwhelming, you might want to start with just a paragraph. You may also find it helpful to begin with a rough draft and to rearrange and simplify your map a few times. Be careful not to be too wordy so that you can more easily remember the material included on your map. Acronyms and other memory devices discussed in chapter 5 can also be useful in mapping. Including them when material is very complex or difficult is an added way to reduce and retain information.

Benefits of Mapping

In addition to being a useful reduction technique, mapping has several extra benefits. First, mapping is a practical method to check your understanding of the relationships among ideas. If you are confused about connections between points, the process of constructing maps will identify fallacies in your reasoning and help you clear up misconceptions.

Second, mapping enhances memory because it requires additional processing of information to create meaningful associations between words and visuals. This transfer of information from words to pictures requires a heightened level of understanding. Words are fairly abstract or theoretical. Sometimes their relationship to actual objects is unclear, especially if the words represent concepts that are new to the learner. Pictures, on the other hand, are closer to the real thing.

Also, it is believed that the left hemisphere of the human brain records written words, while the right hemisphere records visual images. When you map information, you utilize both hemispheres of your brain and, in essence, double your chances of remembering. In addition, students who learn best by visualizing find mapping particularly powerful. When they have difficulty mastering textbook material, creating maps helps them process information for initial understanding, while the visuals serve as memory cues for retention of the material.

Still another benefit of mapping is that it displays both the "big picture" and the relationship of the parts to the whole. Educators advocate viewing the material you want to learn in its entirety, analyzing its various parts, then viewing the information as a whole again. Mapping effectively incorporates this process.

Finally, because the process of mapping is both creative and individualistic, many students find this reduction form stimulating and satisfying. To their surprise, they are able to learn textbook material in a fun way.

Summary

Since memorizing all your reading assignments is far too time-consuming, reducing textbook chapters to only the most important information is a wise college survival skill. Both post-viewing and answering questions assist you in your chapter reduction. This chapter presented four of the most common reduction techniques: making outlines, taking notes, writing summaries, and creating maps. There are unique benefits to each of them, so it is best to experiment and see which one(s) work best for you.

Review Questions

1. Discuss how post-viewing is different from previewing and how it can enhance comprehension.

2. Why is searching for answers to chapter questions without reading the textbook chapter not a good idea?

3. Why does organizing information make it easier to learn? Give an example of course material you might organize to remember for your next exam, and describe how you might organize it.

4. Describe the important characteristics of outlining.

5. List two ways you might use outlining in your college courses.

6. Describe Cornell Notes. Draw a sample Cornell Notes page, and label the different sections.

7. List three general note-taking tips. Identify one that you plan to use and tell why.

8. What are three guidelines for writing summaries? List two ways that the ability to summarize would be helpful in your education.

9. Describe mapping and discuss how it is different from outlining.

10. List three benefits of mapping and describe one way you would practice using it.

Metacognitive Insights

The *Reduce* stage helps you identify and organize key information to remember. Complete the following sentences. On the remaining lines add additional information that you have learned about yourself as you have read the chapter and completed the activities.

1. For me, post-viewing is _____

_____

_____

2. Organizing information _____

_____

_____

3. My favorite reduction technique is _____ because _____

_____

_____

ADDITIONAL INSIGHTS

_____

_____

_____

_____

_____

_____

_____

_____

Retain

- Teach Someone

- Study in Groups

- Recreate in Writing

- Make Study Cards

- Use Mnemonics

- Rehearse

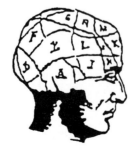

RETAINING THE KEY INFORMATION

There is no single "secret" to a good memory. Many techniques and systems can serve as tools to build an effective memory and enable us to do amazing things.

Kenneth L. Higbee
YOUR MEMORY

For some students, completing the first three stages in BICUM is sufficient. After (1) getting ready to read, (2) reading for meaning, and (3) reducing the key information, they know the material well and will remember it for later use. More students, however, would benefit from using one or more strategies from the fourth stage: the *Retain* stage. Even though comprehension of academic material is usually necessary for learning it, understanding and reducing the material does not guarantee that you will remember it. Preparing outlines, notes, summaries, or maps aids your understanding but does not ensure that the information will be there when you need it. Using other memory techniques can help to permanently secure important material in your mind.

Magazine and television commercials frequently feature enterprising companies claiming to have the secret formula for developing a flawless memory. You have probably seen or heard such ads, and although these advertisements often exaggerate the results of memory training, most people really can make a dramatic difference in how well they remember. And it is not necessary to purchase a high-cost memory package in order to make these changes. Improving your memory is quite possible if you faithfully follow a few time-proven memory techniques. The *Retain* stage offers a variety of these powerful strategies.

How Your Mind Works

Your mind is a storehouse of memories, a reservoir of information. Have you ever wondered how it works? From the beginning of recorded history, people have studied the mind, yet, after hundreds of years of investigation, no one really knows for sure how learning actually takes place. Nevertheless, there are numerous reasonable theories about memory development.

An often used analogy, based on one such theory, is to compare the mind to a computer. For example, a computer translates keystrokes into an electronic language; likewise, your brain changes sensory information into neural language. Also, just as computers can have temporary documents that may or may not be saved, the mind can hold information temporarily. If information is not properly stored in the brain or filed and saved in the computer, it will be lost. A computer can permanently store large amounts of data on disks, hard drives, or CD ROMS. From these information storehouses, computers can retrieve files. Similarly, if material is organized and processed properly, your brain can store vast amounts of information for indefinite periods of time. From this memory storehouse, you can retrieve information into an active working memory (Meyers, 1995).

Like a computer, your memory must accomplish three basic tasks in order to remember an event or an idea: (1) encoding: entering information into your brain, (2) storage: retaining information over periods of time, and (3) retrieval: locating and accessing specific information when needed. Each of these tasks is essential to the memory process, and problems in any of these areas can interfere with your success in remembering information (Baron, 1992).

In 1968, Atkinson and Shiffrin proposed one widely accepted model of human memory (1968). This theory is still useful as a starting place in understanding how the mind works. These researchers suggested that memory is actually three distinct systems: the sensory store, the short-term memory, and the long-term memory. Note the visual that follows.

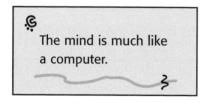

The mind is much like a computer.

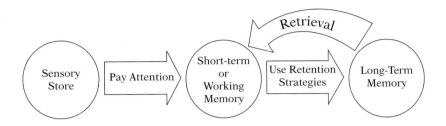

The Sensory Store

The sensory store, the system that encodes information into your brain, is active from the moment you awaken, continuously receiving stimuli from your senses. For instance, while sitting in a class lecture, you intentionally try to listen to the words of your professor. At the same time and without conscious effort on your part, your sensory store also notices the flow of air from the vents in the room and/or the fragrance of the cologne worn by another student. Evidence suggests that the capacity of the sensory store is quite large; that it is capable of encoding virtually everything you see, hear, taste, feel, or smell (Reeves & Sperling, 1986). However, this memory system only holds information briefly, usually a few seconds or less, and without focused attention on your part, you will forget most of this data.

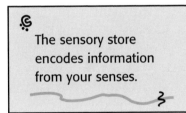

The sensory store encodes information from your senses.

Short-Term Memory

The short-term memory is the next system to come into play. If you notice what your instructor is saying, or if you focus on a particular idea in a textbook, your mind immediately sends the information into your short-term memory, sometimes called the working memory. This memory system has three distinctive characteristics that are worth knowing about. First, as its name suggests, the short-term memory does not last very long. Unless you actively repeat information in this memory system, it will fade quickly, in as little as twenty seconds (Peterson & Peterson, 1959). Second, it has a limited capacity, usually only seven separate items, plus or minus two. Sometimes referred to as *Miller's Magic 7*, named for the researcher who determined this number, this landmark research, although documented many years ago, is still considered valid today (Miller, 1956). A common example of this principle is the use of the seven digit phone number.

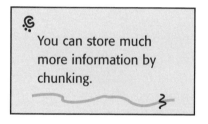

Short-term memory doesn't last long and has limited capacity for information.

By grouping or chunking information, it is possible to store more than seven individual items in the short-term memory. Your mind can hold chunks of information just as easily as individual details. Recall the discussion in chapter 4 about "Organized Information." Organized information is easier to memorize than strings of information. This is especially true when considering the limits of the short-term memory system. For example, read the following group of letters, then cover them up and try to repeat them from memory: IBMNBATWAFBI. Were you successful? Probably not. Now read the same group of letters organized or divided into recognizable clusters: IBM, NBA, TWA, FBI. Try to recall them now. Were you successful this time? You probably succeeded because the chunking helped you recognize that these letters represent well-known organizations. With the help of chunking, your short-term memory can actually hold much more information.

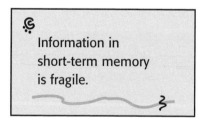

You can store much more information by chunking.

Third, the short-term memory is susceptible to interference; that is, additional incoming information or stressful circumstances can easily displace information already in the system (Reitman, 1974). Another way of saying this is that information in this system is fragile; it can easily be forgotten. This is one reason why cramming for tests is not a good idea. Stuffing information into your short-term memory can easily result in forgetting the information when you need it the most, which is often during an exam.

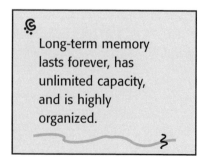

Information in short-term memory is fragile.

Long-Term Memory

The third memory system is the long-term memory. It stores your childhood memories, your accumulated knowledge, and any information that you learned over time. This memory system has some very useful characteristics. For one thing, there is ample evidence that it lasts forever. Even if you have difficulty retrieving information from your

Long-term memory lasts forever, has unlimited capacity, and is highly organized.

long-term memory, it never really disappears. Second, this system appears to have an unlimited capacity for storing information. Many experts maintain that there is never a time when you will fill the storage vault in your long-term memory. The third characteristic is that this memory system is highly organized. Information is not randomly placed; rather, it is filed in hierarchical categories according to related information and meaningful concepts (Ellis, 1997). Remember that once information is placed in the long-term memory, it must then be accessible to be retrieved when the need arises. Consciously filing information in an organized manner can improve your chances of finding it when you want it.

Moving information from the short-term to the long-term memory is what the *Retain* stage is all about. As you practice the following strategies, remember that once your sensory store encodes information, you must pay attention in order to transfer the information to your short-term or working memory. Once the information is in your short-term memory, it will only last a limited time unless you use strategies to transfer it into your permanent long-term memory.

If you actively use your metacognitive skills, you will notice that some memory techniques seem more natural and that you get better results when using them than when you use other ones. Also, recognize that you do not have to use all the strategies in this stage in order to improve your memory. However, try each one before you decide which strategies to use regularly and which ones to file away for later use. The strategies in this stage are not listed in any particular order of use or importance. Each strategy, though, has been practiced by thousands of students and has proven to be worthwhile.

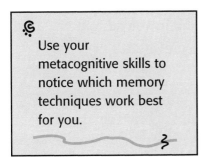

Moving information from the short-term to the long-term memory is what the *Retain* stage is all about.

Use your metacognitive skills to notice which memory techniques work best for you.

Teach Someone

Did you know that teachers can benefit from their own lectures? As they share information with their students, teachers can actually improve their own understanding and retention of the material. Sounds surprising, doesn't it? Research shows that the process of teaching is in itself a

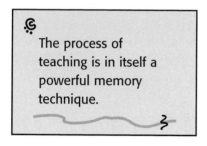

The process of teaching is in itself a powerful memory technique.

Using several senses makes a deeper impression on the brain.

powerful memory technique. Walter Gong, a great educator, once said that to learn something well, teach it to someone else.

One method to improve your retention of textbook information, then, is to teach someone. Look for specific opportunities to share with others the information you want to remember. That is, whenever you learn something you want to keep in your memory, explain the information to someone else. Perhaps you do this naturally; many students do. If you do, begin to notice how this technique influences your retention of material. However, if teaching others is not something you normally do, make the decision now to try. You can expect teaching to help you clarify, reinforce, and, in many instances, lock the information into your own memory. There are several reasons that teaching contributes to retention.

Usually, teaching someone involves speaking aloud. You learned in the *Read* stage that a useful fix-up strategy is to read out loud. Just hearing your own voice can help you understand difficult material that was confusing when you read it silently. Speaking aloud can also be a powerful memory technique. When you vocalize, you use several different senses. First, your eyes focus on the words. Second, there is the physical sensation in your throat, tongue, and lips as you say the words. Also, you hear the sounds. Actually, the activities of thinking, pronouncing, and hearing your own voice involve your body, as well as your mind, in the learning process. Combining the use of several senses makes a deeper impression on the brain than using them separately.

Another reason teaching is so powerful is that it forces you to organize your thoughts in a meaningful way. If your explanation of an idea is unclear, the person you are teaching will probably question your reasoning and ask you to explain further. For example, if you tried to explain Roosevelt's New Deal to a friend and were not certain what reforms were involved, your friend would likely recognize your confusion. If you searched your textbook for this information and then made certain your explanation was clear, you would more likely remember the reforms.

If your friends are unavailable when you want to teach someone, try getting together with an absent student. This could benefit both of you. Some students report positive experiences from teaching family members. One student reported the following experience:

> I decided to "teach" my eighteen-month-old daughter diesel mechanics. I held my daughter for hours discussing the material with her. She loved the attention from her dad, and I was totally amazed at how much I remembered.

Study in Groups

You just learned about the benefits of hearing your own voice while teaching someone. Group study takes the advantages of this technique and combines them with the strength of group association. The social aspects of learning with others can be remarkably motivating for some

---

METACOGNITIVE TRAINING ACTIVITY
Teach Someone
·ᔔ· MTA 5.1 ·ᔔ·

⅜ DIRECTIONS:
Ask a classmate to be a study partner.
Arrange to teach him/her a portion of the material you both need to know for an exam.
Evaluate the teaching experience by responding to the following items.

1. Record the name of the course that you and the student are studying.

2. Describe three of the ideas you taught your study partner.

3. Discuss the value of using this assignment as a means of understanding and remembering what you are learning. Include what went well and what you would change if you were to use this method again.

4. Self grade _____% and brief justification.

---

students. For many students, studying with fellow students is much more conducive to learning than isolating themselves in the library. Discussing concepts within a group is often more memorable and energizing than merely mulling ideas over in your own mind.

Also, working with students who are in the same classes with you and who are responsible for the same material is usually more useful than just teaching an accommodating roommate. Sometimes finding friends or family members to listen to you teach is difficult; they can be either too busy with their own studying or are not interested in the subject you want to teach. Even the best of friends might be reluctant to be attentive for hours to topics that are unfamiliar and that are not naturally of interest to them. In contrast, students in the same class who participate in study groups have the common goal of succeeding on their exams. Teaching and sharing with others in study groups can be a productive experience.

Forming Study Groups

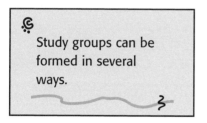

Study groups can be formed in several ways.

Study groups can be formed in several ways. Sometimes instructors create study groups within their classes. Often they consider specific student characteristics and/or abilities as they form these groups. If the strengths and weaknesses of the students in a study group complement each other, the results should be very positive and productive. If you are fortunate enough to be in a class where groups are teacher-created, take full advantage of this learning opportunity.

Also, study groups offered by college tutoring services and directed by trained tutors can be very helpful. If you join such a group, be sure to participate actively rather than sitting back and passively observing. Remember, experts say you will retain about 95 percent of what you teach. Actively participating in groups gives you an opportunity to teach. Retention from just listening is often only about 10 percent.

If neither of the above group study options is available, you can form your own study groups. Identify which of your classmates are motivated and committed to doing well. Usually these are the students who score high on tests and assignments. Invite some of them to join you as you study. Recognize, however, that studying in groups does not always ensure that your memory of course information will improve. In fact, sometimes study groups can interfere with retention of material, especially if the meetings turn into social gatherings.

Study Group Guidelines

Agreeing to some guidelines at the start of your study sessions will increase your chances of success and ward off potential problems that may arise later. The following suggestions have been useful for many students and may help you have a productive experience with group study.

1. Check to see if your schedules coordinate. Arrange specific times and places to meet.

2. As a group, select a leader who will be in charge of contacting members.

3. Determine whether to divide the reading assignment among the group members or to have everyone read the entire assignment. (The latter is usually preferred—it ensures that everyone has some basic understanding of the material.)

4. Identify a section of the assignment for each member to study in depth and prepare to teach to the group.

5. Agree that everyone must attend class lectures and take quality notes, as well as attend all study sessions and come fully prepared.

6. Take turns teaching the assigned parts of the text.

7. Compare and share class notes.

8. As a group, identify other effective ways to master the textbook material.

9. Have a goal or agenda for each meeting.

By following these and other guidelines that you may decide are necessary, your study sessions can be productive, and you should improve your memory of the class material.

METACOGNITIVE TRAINING ACTIVITY
Study in a Group
·ᴕ· MTA 5.2 ·ᴕ·

ᶾ DIRECTIONS:

In one of your courses, form a study group for the next exam. Answer the following questions about your experience with the group.

1. How many were in your group, and how did you form it?

2. Where, when, and how often did you meet?

3. Explain how well you and the group were able to stay focused on the course material during the study session.

4. How was the study group conducted? For example:

   a. Was the reading assignment divided among group members?

   b. Did you take turns teaching sections of the material?

5. Would you want to study with the same people again? Why or why not?

6. Self grade _____% and brief justification.

Recreate in Writing

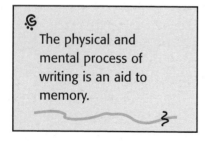

The physical and mental process of writing is an aid to memory.

For many students, the physical and mental process of writing is an aid to memory. By being more aware of how you learn, you can decide whether writing is beneficial for you. Try rewriting your outline, notes, summary, or maps to see if this procedure helps you better remember the information. Be sure to focus on the content while you process and copy the words. Do not fool yourself into thinking that writing without focused attention is helpful. For most students, such a practice is a total waste of time. Instead, as you write remind yourself of the main points and their supports so you will build relationships among the ideas you record.

Even better than just copying your reduced form is to recreate it as much as possible from memory. Start with the most important ideas first; then fill in the specifics as you go. Refer back to your original reduced form as needed. Some students rewrite their reduced forms, or at least part of them, several times in an effort to make the information permanent. Use this writing strategy as frequently as you find it useful. Eventually, you should be able to reproduce your reduced form almost, if not completely, from memory. This is called **blank page testing.** When you do this, you are processing information at a deeper and more stable level of learning. You are also simulating testing conditions, which gives you a good check of what you know.

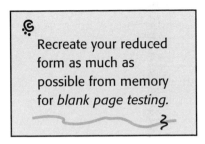

Recreate your reduced form as much as possible from memory for *blank page testing.*

Recognition Versus Recall Level Learning

The idea that there are different levels of learning is widely accepted by educators. Two of the most commonly proposed levels are recognition and recall. Repetition alone usually only results in **recognition** level learning, or cue-dependent knowledge, which is only minimally useful. It helps students pick out answers on some multiple choice and true/false tests. Unfortunately, even on these kinds of tests, dependence on cues can prove disastrous when the information is reworded or when the needed hints are not included. Also, successful performance on short answer or essay tests is almost impossible with this low level of learning. In short, recognition level learning, which is achieved through repetition of information, is simply not adequate preparation for test taking.

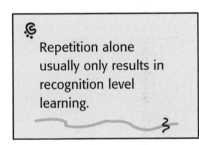

Repetition alone usually only results in recognition level learning.

Also, when information is learned only to the recognition level, your ability to recall it often lasts only long enough to complete a test. Recognition-level learning makes you very susceptible to test anxiety. When you become nervous during exams, you are likely to forget the information you thought you had learned.

A more dependable and permanent way of learning is to master the material to the **recall** level, a memory level that is not as dependent on visual cues. Learning to this level is very useful for any exam preparation but is essential for short answer and essay tests. The technique mentioned

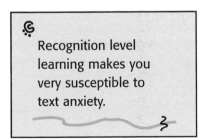

Recognition level learning makes you very susceptible to text anxiety.

earlier, blank page testing, checks to see if you have learned material to the written recall level. Although testing for recall can also be done in your head or out loud, depending on your needs and circumstances, often this strategy is not as effective. Several of the strategies that will be discussed in this chapter, such as the split-page testing method and flash cards, require recall level learning.

Split-Page Testing

One very effective method of recreating in writing is a method called **split-page testing.** To use this method, fold a sheet of paper lengthwise, as shown in Figure 5.1 (p. 151). Then read a section or a chapter from a textbook, and create test questions you think may appear on the exam. The questions are on the left side of the page and the answers are directly across from them on the right. To use these questions as a test, you can either fold the right side under or cut it off. You can then write out the answers on a blank sheet of paper.

Perhaps the most important benefit of this method is that it helps students learn to think like college professors do when creating exams. Learning to anticipate what professors will cover and the kinds of questions they will ask can be an important part of successful testing.

Some kinds of questions, such as those asking for simple definitions of terms, are usually considered *literal questions.* True/false or multiple-choice questions are frequently used to test literal information. However, most college exams will also include the use of higher level questions that require making inferences and applying principles to new situations.

Inference and application questions are often more difficult to answer and can usually be found on essay and short answer exams. As a rule these kinds of exam questions contain fewer cues for you to rely on and require more critical thinking skills.

Besides helping you learn to think as teachers do, another benefit of this method is that it reduces test anxiety by providing you with a trial run. As you find that you can master material and successfully reproduce information in writing, your confidence will grow.

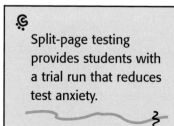

Split-page testing provides students with a trial run that reduces test anxiety.

An added advantage of split-page testing is that you can exchange the questions and answers with classmates. The original answers can be folded under or cut off and used as an answer key. This gives additional practice by increasing the number of questions you have been exposed to as you prepare for exams. A broader understanding of the material can be achieved by this collective effort.

The sample split-page questions in Figure 5.1 are based on the previously discussed article in chapter 4 on "The

Sample Split-Page for "The Roots of American Government"

Questions	Answers
1. What is common law?	1. A form of government guaranteeing trial by jury and protection of fundamental rights.
2. What was the basis for John Locke's theories on government?	2. The roots for Locke's theories came from the Greeks and Romans.
3. Why did Locke believe that certain rights were inalienable?	3. He believed that rights to life, liberty, and happiness were natural, not government's to give or take away.
4. What was the Enlightenment?	4. An 18th century movement that sought to understand the proper order of nature and society.
5. Did Locke's ideas help bring about the American Revolution? Would his theories justify future revolutions? Why or why not?	5. Yes, because he greatly influenced the American Declaration of Independence and his theories give justification for rebelling against unjust governments.

FIGURE 5.1 SAMPLE SPLIT-PAGE TESTING

Roots of American Government" (p. 111). Notice which questions are literal and which ones require inference and application.

After carefully studying the questions and answers in Figure 5.1, have you determined which two questions are literal? If you answered questions 1 and 4, you are correct. The answers to these questions can be found and underlined in the article in Figure 4.1.

Question 2 is almost literal, but a bit of interpretation is required. You must conclude that the words "roots" and "basis" of John Locke's theories are used synonymously. If you do this, then you can readily determine the correct answer.

Questions 3 and 5 require some interpretation. The word *inalienable* may or may not be familiar to you. If it is not, then you may need to ask someone what it means or look it up in the dictionary. One dictionary defines "inalienable rights" as those that cannot be taken away. Locke therefore believed in rights that were natural and not government's to give or take away.

Question 5 also requires some application of knowledge beyond that stated in Figure 4.1. If Locke's ideas influenced Thomas Jefferson, the major author of the Declaration of Independence, they also helped the Americans feel justified in rebelling against an oppressive British government. (Some background knowledge may be required at this point to know how Great Britain had infringed on the Americans' inalienable rights.) Therefore, it follows that Locke's ideas would likewise justify other countries in similar situations to rebel.

If you take the time to predict and thoughtfully construct test questions and answers, you will probably find yourself much better prepared for exams. You will be pleased and surprised to find that many of your questions actually appear on professors' tests. Learning to think as college professors do can be a very empowering process. Using the split-page testing method can be like a dress rehearsal for exams, usually with excellent results.

To strengthen this memory process, consider answering the questions out loud as you reproduce them in writing. If you do this, you will be combining three senses: sight, touch, and sound. Multi-sensory input increases your chances of remembering.

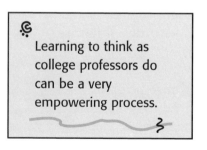

Learning to think as college professors do can be a very empowering process.

METACOGNITIVE TRAINING ACTIVITY
Recreate in Writing
·ᘒ· MTA 5.3 ·ᘒ·

⅗ DIRECTIONS:
Reproduce one of the following: an outline, Cornell notes, a
   summary, or a map.
Respond to the following items.

---

1. On a blank sheet of paper, try to reproduce your material from
   memory.

2. About how much were you able to recall? Give a percentage.

3. Write three or four sentences discussing the effectiveness of this
   strategy for you.

4. What suggestions would you give to other students as they
   prepare to complete this activity?

5. Self grade _____% and brief justification.

Make Study Cards

Creating the right kind of **study cards** to fit each type of information can be one of the most effective techniques available to you. By creating your cards right after you preview a chapter, you can become very proficient at predicting what will appear on your exams. To be the most effective, your study cards will need to grow and evolve as your knowledge of the material increases.

What this means is that after an overview of a chapter, you will already have some idea of what the author thinks is most important. The headings, subheadings, and other bolded or italicized information has already been selected and designated by the author(s) as ideas worth your notice. Right after your preview, if you begin to place these key terms and concepts on study cards, your chances of success on your next exam have already increased. Since words alone involve mostly abstract thinking, just the simple task of adding a visual to your word cards will make a more

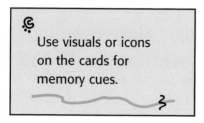

Use visuals or icons on the cards for memory cues.

lasting impression on your memory. The visuals or icons on your cards will also serve as memory cues when you are practicing or rehearsing. As you picture your visual in your mind and make a meaningful association with the concepts you are trying to learn, the mental image will help you define the term or answer your question(s).

For an example of this concept, see the first set of cards in Figure 5.2. Although *philanthropist* is a rather long and sometimes confusing word, the picture shows the two important parts of the word's meaning. The heart symbolizes the love of mankind and the $ reminds us that a philanthropist often gives donations to charitable causes. This is a word that might appear in a sociology or psychology text, and placing *philanthropist* on a card will help transfer its meaning into your lasting, long-term memory.

The second set of cards in Figure 5.2 shows how a basic vocabulary card can be enhanced and made more meaningful by asking additional questions about the biology term *planarian*. Not only will this help you learn what that word means, but it will give you a chance to learn related concepts such as the order and class. By wording the card as a question, you are actually having a chance to practice answering questions for a quiz or an exam. The more you practice in advance, the more information you will have in the stable long-term memory, and the less chance there will be for test anxiety.

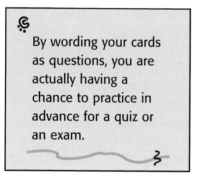

By wording your cards as questions, you are actually having a chance to practice in advance for a quiz or an exam.

The third and fourth sets of cards in Figure 5.2 are called **Double Question Q-Cards.** Although higher levels of thinking are required to create this kind of card, the advantages are often increased as well. First of all, the creation of these cards can bring you to a more complete understanding of the concepts you are learning. You are also less likely to be surprised by exam questions that are worded in unusual ways because you have practiced wording your questions in different ways as well. Another benefit of thinking about terms and concepts from different angles is the greater likelihood of storing memories in different locations in your brain.

Although the sample Q-Cards in Figure 5.2 do not have visuals, adding pictures to them would be the next step to enhance their power. The fact that cards can be so versatile is one of their greatest advantages.

Philanthropist

World of Words pg 175

 • One Who Loves
mankind and often
proves it by
charitable donations

What Are planarians?
Name the order and class
they belong to.
(plā-Nĕr- Ē-ans)

Source: Biology p615

Def. Any of various flat worms
that prey on tiny invertebrates
or on dead organisms.

Order: Tridaclida
Class: Turbellaria

What Are 3 types
of Monosaccharides
(simple sugar)?

Glucose, Fructose,
And ribose Are
3 examples of
what?

what fuel is required
for photosynthesis
to take place?

CO_2 is A required
fuel for what
vegetative chemical
process?

FIGURE 5.2 SAMPLE OF STUDY CARDS

Advantages Of Using Study Cards

Besides being a valuable tool to help you learn information to the recall level, study cards have several additional benefits. First, they allow you to break information into manageable pieces. Large amounts of material can seem less intimidating when you face one segment at a time. Second, study cards are especially conducive to mastering the large volume of new vocabulary associated with many introductory level content courses such as psychology or biology. Third, study cards are "portable"; that is, they are convenient to carry around and can be used during the many "wait times" that are part of most students' lives. For example, while waiting for a class to begin, waiting in line at a bank, or while riding a bus, you can review your study cards. Securing the cards with a rubber band or a ring to keep them together is also a good idea.

To use your study cards to their greatest advantage, first read the information (the "cue") on one side of the cards; then try to say or write a response to the cue. Then turn the card over to check your answer. Repeat this process until you can easily produce accurate responses.

To make this strategy more powerful, use tally marks to monitor how many times you have to view the card to learn the contents. Simply place a tally mark on the bottom of the card each time you attempt a response. When you can accurately respond to the other side of the card without turning it over, remove it from the stack. Concentrate on reducing the number of cards in the stack you don't know.

Next try switching the sides of the cards you read. For example, read the definitions and see if you can remember what words they are defining, or read the answers to your questions and see if you can recreate the questions. By testing yourself with both questions and answers, you will be prepared for a variety of testing formats.

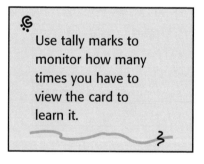

Study cards help break large learning tasks into manageable pieces.

Use tally marks to monitor how many times you have to view the card to learn it.

METACOGNITIVE TRAINING ACTIVITY
Make Study Cards
·ɞ· MTA 5.4 ·ɞ·

ɞ DIRECTIONS:

After creating study cards and using them to learn the material for an exam, evaluate your effectiveness by answering the following questions.

1. Create at least 10 study cards, and use them to learn material for your next exam. Draw visuals on five or more of the cards.

2. Discuss how and when you used the cards to test yourself.

3. After taking the examination on the material, discuss how effective the cards were in helping you to recall the information.

4. Self grade _____% and brief justification.

Use Mnemonics

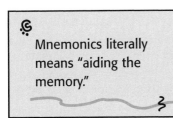

Mnemonics literally means "aiding the memory."

Pictures are inherently more memorable than words alone.

The term **mnemonics**, sometimes used to refer to unusual, creative and/or artificial memory tricks, literally means "aiding the memory." The use of mnemonics can help you secure information in your memory that you might otherwise forget. These memory aids are often based on two well-known memory principles: **association** and **visualization**. Association involves relating new information to be learned to information you already know. For example, to distinguish between stalactites and stalagmites, remember that stala**c**tites hang from the **c**eiling and stala**g**mites project from the **g**round. By associating the bolded letters in these new words with words you already know, "ceiling" and "ground," you can more easily recall the difference between these names for cavern deposits.

The other principle is **visualization,** creating specific mental imagery of the information you want to learn. Visualization enhances memory because pictures are inherently more memorable than words alone. Words that create images are coded in both the verbal and visual memory and thus are twice as likely to be recalled when needed. Common examples of mnemonics that use these principles include rhymes, acronyms, and acrostics.

Rhymes

Do you remember the date that Columbus reportedly discovered America? Most likely, you answered "1492." How did you recall that information? You probably knew this date because you learned it in the rhyme "In fourteen hundred and ninety-two, Columbus sailed the ocean blue . . ."

Now answer this question, "What year did the Vikings probably land on American soil?" Unless you are a history buff, you likely do not know the answer. The main difference between knowing and not knowing these historical dates is their connection to rhymes. If you had learned a rhyme about the Vikings landing in America, you would have been able to respond with the same ease that you replied to the question about Columbus. Likewise, do you remember the rule for spelling words that have "ie" in them? Many of you will quickly reply "**I** before **E**, except after **C**, or when sounds like **A**, as in neighbor or weigh." By recalling this rule and remembering the few exceptions, you can spell most "ie" words correctly.

You can use this rhyming technique to help you remember textbook material. Just make up a simple jingle with the material you need to learn. For example, the acronym RAPPS was created by taking the first letter of each of the five freedoms listed in the First Amendment of the Constitution (**R**eligion, **A**ssembly, **P**etition, **P**ress and **S**peech). The following rhyme or rap also helps in remembering these freedoms:

Speakin' of freedoms, oh what could they be?

Freedom of **R**eligion and **A**ssembly

Freedom of **P**etition and Freedom of **P**ress,

Freedom of **S**peech, now don't distress.

As you can see from this example, the rhymes you make up do not have to be polished pieces of poetry but can still help to increase your chances of doing well on tests. So keep your rhymes simple, but be certain you make them meaningful. Including humor in your verses may increase the effectiveness of this technique.

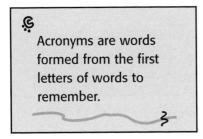

Acronyms are words formed from the first letters of words to remember.

Acronyms

Acronyms, words formed from the first letters of words you want to remember, are another mnemonic. The study-reading plan you are learning in this book is referred to by the acronym BICUM. Acronyms are quite popular. Do you recognize these well-known acronyms: NASA, SCUBA, and AIDS? If you knew that NASA means "**N**ational **A**eronautics and **S**pace **A**dministration, SCUBA stands for **S**elf-**C**ontained **U**nderwater **B**reathing **A**pparatus, and AIDS is an acronym for **A**cquired **I**mmune **D**eficiency **S**yndrome," then you are correct.

Acronyms are useful because they can help you recall lists of words you need to remember. Have you had the experience of needing to know several terms for a test and being able to recall only part of them? Then later with the test behind you, you could easily remember the information. Acronyms can help you avoid this frustrating situation. They can serve as hooks to pull information from your memory that you otherwise might not be able to retrieve.

Knowing specific study acronyms could help you answer the following questions. See how well you do. "What are the names of the five Great Lakes?"

Do you remember only one or two of the five? The acronym HOMES may help you recall the other names. The **H** stands for _____. Yes, **H**uron. The **O** stands for _____. Yes, **O**ntario. See how easily you can recall information with the help of an acronym? The names of the other Great Lakes are **M**ichigan, **E**rie, and **S**uperior.

If you read music, you probably learned an acronym to remember the following information: What are the space notes in order in the treble clef? Many of you immediately recalled the word FACE and remembered that the notes in the spaces are **F**, **A**, **C**, and **E**. This acronym has helped thousands of beginning music students learn this basic information.

Another well-known acronym used by students in science classes is ROY G. BIV. The name stands for the colors of the rainbow or the light spectrum: **R**ed, **O**range, **Y**ellow, **G**reen, **B**lue, **I**ndigo and **V**iolet. Biology and anatomy students usually have to remember a vast amount of information. Memorizing the organs in the various body systems is one commonly assigned task. A popular acronym to help students remember the organs in the excretory system is SKILL (**S**kin, **K**idneys, **I**ntestines, **L**iver, and **L**ungs).

You do not have to depend on acronyms that other people have created. Actually taking the time and creative energy to create your own acronyms makes them more effective as memory cues. Follow the easy steps listed below to practice creating these memory aids.

1. Take the beginning letter of each of the key words you want to remember and create a word. If the order of the words is not important, switch the letters around until you form a word or an arrangement of letters that looks like a word. You do not have to make a real word.

2. Include a vowel in each syllable so you can pronounce the word you create. If you do not have enough words you may add vowels to your acronym to form a word. Writing these added vowels in lower case letters will help you remember that they are included only for pronunciation purposes. For example, the word "HUNTeR" could be used as an acronym to remember the following socioeconomic terms: **H**omeless, **U**pperclass, **N**eighbors, **T**ransients, and **R**enegades. Notice that the **e** is lowercase because it does not represent a term that needs to be remembered, but all the capitalized letters in the word stand for socioeconomic terms describing various groups in our society.

3. Make a firm association between the acronym and the information you need to remember. Simply creating an acronym without connecting it to information is a waste of time. Build this connection by writing the

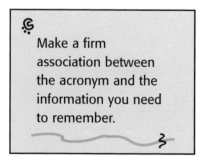

Creating your own acronyms makes them more effective as memory cues.

Make a firm association between the acronym and the information you need to remember.

information you need to remember using only the acronym you created as a clue. For example, see if you remember the organs of the excretory system by filling in the blanks after the letters in the acronym SKILL.

S _____ **K** _____ **I** _____ **L** _____ **L** _____

(Refer to the list of organs mentioned a few paragraphs earlier to see if you are correct.) Repeating this process several times will strengthen the connection between your acronym and the material you need to remember.

Acrostics

Acrostics are memory aids that use a series of words in which the first letter in each word is used to form phrases or sentences. These are often popular with students. Similar to acronyms, they also can serve as hooks to pull information from your memory. There are many common acrostics. The sentence **E**very **G**ood **B**oy **D**oes **F**ine is an acrostic that helps students remember the lines of the treble clef (E, G, B, D, and F). Likewise, many math students are grateful for the sentence, **P**lease **E**xcuse **M**y **D**ear **A**unt **S**ally when they are solving algebraic equations. These words represent the order of operations: **P**arenthesis, **E**xponents, **M**ultiplication or **D**ivision, **A**ddition or **S**ubtraction. The names of the planets in order from the sun are easy to learn when you remember the sentence, **M**y **V**ery **E**legant **M**other **J**ust **S**erved **U**s **N**ine **P**izzas. The first letter of each word in that sentence stands for the following planets: **M**ercury, **V**enus, **E**arth, **M**ars, **J**upiter, **S**aturn, **U**ranus, **N**eptune, and **P**luto.

Anatomy students use this acrostic: **O**n **O**ld **O**lympus' **T**owering **T**op, **A** **F**inn **A**nd **G**erman **V**iewed **S**ome **H**erds. The students then picture a mountain called Olympus with a Finn and a German on the top looking at a herd (of reindeer perhaps). This highly visual sentence would be connected to the following cranial nerves: **O**lfactory, **O**ptic, **O**culomotor, **T**rochlear, **T**rigeminal, **A**bducens, **F**acial, **A**uditory, **G**lossopharyngeal, **V**agus, **S**pinal accessory, and **H**ypoglossal.

The steps for creating acrostics are similar to those for creating acronyms. If necessary, refer back to the information on acronyms; then follow these three basic steps.

1. Select words that begin with the first letter of each point of information you want to remember and create a sentence.

2. Add words if the information you want to learn does not begin with the letters you need for your sentence. Just write the "helping words" in lower case letters so that you do not confuse them with the other words.

3. Establish a firm connection between the information you want to remember and the words in the sentence that you created.

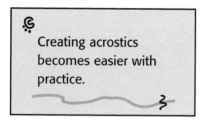

Creating acrostics becomes easier with practice.

Creating acrostics becomes easier with practice. Once you begin, you will find many uses for this type of mnemonic. You can use them in conjunction with or instead of acronyms. For instance, sometimes you might have difficulty creating an acronym, but an acrostic would be easier. In general, acrostics work better for longer information.

You can hook several sentences together if you need to learn a longer list of information. For example, the following acrostic can help you remember the thirteen original colonies, which are: **V**irginia, **M**assachusetts, **N**ew **H**ampshire, **N**ew **Y**ork, **C**onnecticut, **M**aryland, **R**hode **I**sland, **D**elaware, **P**ennsylvania, **N**orth **C**arolina, **N**ew **J**ersey, **S**outh **C**arolina, **G**eorgia.

> **V**irginia **M**akes **N**utritious **H**amburgers.
>
> **N**ice **Y**oung **C**onnie **M**akes **R**ather **I**mpressive **D**oughnuts.
>
> **P**enny **N**ever **C**ooks **N**oodles, **J**ust **S**weet **C**runchy **G**ranola.

Notice that this acrostic did not require any extra words to improve the flow of the sentences. Each word is attached to the name of one of the original colonies.

Have fun creating acrostics; make your sentences depict silly, exciting, or unusual pictures or ideas. Actually, if your acrostics are ridiculous, action-packed, or a bit strange, you are more likely to remember them. The human mind forgets ordinary, boring material much more readily than interesting, unusual information. Do not forget to associate the information you want to remember with your mnemonic. Acrostics are useless without a clear connection to the information you want to remember.

Mini Stories

Mini stories are mnemonics that you have probably used from childhood without even realizing you were practicing powerful memory aids. Most people naturally remember information that is presented in story form. Stories are really just extensions of acrostics. Just create visual sentences using the beginning letters of the information you want to learn and weave them together to form a connecting story. For example, look at the list of the presidents of the United States and then use the story that follows to memorize them.

Washington, **A**dams, **J**efferson, **M**adison, **M**onroe, **A**dams, **J**ackson, **V**an **B**uren, **H**arrison, **T**yler, **P**olk, **T**aylor, **F**illmore, **P**ierce, **B**uchanan, **L**incoln, **J**ohnson, **G**rant, **H**ayes, **G**arfield, **A**rthur, **C**leveland, **H**arrison, **C**leveland, **M**cKinley, **R**oosevelt, **T**aft, **W**ilson, **H**arding, **C**oolidge, **H**oover, **R**oosevelt, **T**ruman, **E**isenhower, **K**ennedy, **J**ohnson, **N**ixon, **F**ord, **C**arter, **R**eagan, **B**ush, **C**linton

While **A**dams **J**umped **M**ini (hurdles), **M**onroe **A**ggressively **J**umped **V**ery **B**ig **H**urdles. **T**yler **P**ushed **T**aylor, **F**ully **P**assing **B**y **L**incoln. **J**ohn **G**rabbed **H**uge **G**arfield **A**nd **C**limbed (over) **H**arry. **C**lever **M**ike **R**an **T**oward **W**illy. **H**arvey **C**ould **H**ardly **R**un **T**oward **E**isen. **K**enny **J**umped **N**ear **F**rank. **C**arter **R**an **B**y **C**lint (and won the race).

Notice that this story has several words in parentheses. These are extra words added to help the flow of the story and therefore do not have names of presidents attached to them. All the other words in the story correspond to presidential names. If you learn this story, be sure to carefully connect each name individually with the word that it corresponds with. Recognize that this story helps you to remember only the last names of the presidents. Since some of the presidents have the same last names, but different first names, you will have to consciously distinguish among these presidents. For example, you will have to remember that John Adams came before J.Q. Adams.

Songs

The sounds and the rhythm in **songs** are especially memorable. You might have had the experience of listening to a song on the radio while dressing for school, then later that day humming the tune or singing the words without even realizing what you were doing. You might have been surprised that you had also memorized the words. Music is readily absorbed by the brain, and the words connected with it can often be easily recalled.

Use this natural memory technique and make up your own simple melody, or pick one from a song you already know. Then connect the information you want to learn to the music. Sing it a few times, and you will probably be pleased at how much you remember. For example, you can memorize the names of the seven continents by putting them to the tune of *Row, Row, Row Your Boat*. Recall the original words of the song: "Row, row, row your boat, gently down the stream. Merrily, merrily, merrily, merrily, life is but a dream." Now substitute the names of the continents for the words of the tune.

> American, North and South, and Antarctica,
> Asia, Europe, Africa, then Australia.

Sing this song a few times, and you will soon have this useful piece of trivia stored in your mind.

Picture Links

You might also try creating **picture links**, or "chaining," as it is sometimes called, as a memory aid. Like the mnemonics discussed previously, picture links are simple to create, and they become even easier to make the more you practice. Use the steps below to try this method of picture linking.

1. Form a mental picture of each item you want to remember.

2. Associate the picture of the first item with the one that follows and so forth.

Make the first visualization especially memorable because it will lead you to the remaining items in your list. Form a mental connection between this item and the second item you want to remember. Each picture you create should serve as a mental "arrow" that directs your mind to the next picture. Follow this same pattern for each additional item in your list. Do not try to connect all of the items together into one big picture. Instead, concentrate on associating two items at a time; then link them together to form a chain. To see how using picture links can help you remember some useful information, study the example below:

Steps in the Writing Process

1. Brainstorm or free write.

2. Develop a thesis or main idea.

3. Find supporting details.

4. Create an outline.

5. Write from the outline.

To remember step number one, brainstorming, visualize thought bubbles, like those used in cartoons. See these appearing one after the other until one starts to illuminate brighter than the others like a light bulb coming on. This image is often associated with a good idea, like a main point as in step number two. For remembering step number three, supporting details, visualize a lamp stand to support the light bulb. For steps four and five, picture the light shining on an outline you are tracing around a body found lying on the floor. See yourself using the chalk you traced with to begin writing.

Peg System

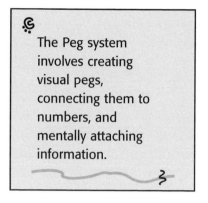

The Peg system involves creating visual pegs, connecting them to numbers, and mentally attaching information.

The **Peg system** utilizes the principle of visualization and is a particularly effective memory technique. The human mind is capable of drawing an unlimited array of visuals, and the process of creating mental pictures helps lock information into memory. This system involves creating a set of visual pegs and connecting them to numbers. Then the information to be remembered is mentally attached to the peg words. The following familiar rhyming words are often used as mental pegs.

1 = bun	6 = sticks
2 = shoe	7 = heaven
3 = tree	8 = gate
4 = door	9 = wine
5 = hive	10 = hen

To connect these words with their rhyming number counterparts, picture specific, familiar items. For example, for number one, picture the first kind of bun that comes to mind, such as a hamburger bun; for number two, picture your own shoe; and for number three, picture a tree you are familiar with, etc. Once these peg words are securely locked in your mind, you can begin to attach information to them.

Read the next few paragraphs with focused attention, associating the visuals described with the peg words to learn the first ten amendments to the U.S. Constitution, known as the Bill of Rights.

1. Freedoms of religion, assembly, petition, press, and speech

2. Right to bear arms

3. Not required to quarter (house) troops (soldiers)

4. Protection from search and seizure

5. Do not have to testify against or incriminate ourselves

6. Right to a speedy trial

7. Right to a trial by jury

8. Protection against cruel and unusual punishment

9. People's rights

10. States' rights

Recall the discussion earlier in this chapter on rhymes. Remember the acronym created to remember the five freedoms in the First Amendment: RAPPS. Here is the rhyme or rap again.

Speakin' of freedoms, oh what could they be

Freedom of Religion and Assembly

Freedom of Petition and Freedom of Press

Freedom of Speech, now don't distress.

1. Now, picture the first peg (bun) saying this rap. Mentally rehearse the words to the rap, and see the bun rocking back and forth, moving to the beat of the rhyme. Repeat this visualization two or three times.

2. Next, move to the Second Amendment, the right to bear arms, and connect this information to the second peg (shoe). See a bear wearing your shoe and holding a gun. Or picture a bear holding several arms in one hand and a shoe in his other hand. Again, review this picture several times to lock it into your memory. Do this for each of the other eight pegs, making certain the pictures are firmly in place before moving to the next information.

3. The third constitutional right is protection from having to quarter soldiers. Picture the third peg (tree), and see yourself emphatically telling the soldiers who have come to your home, demanding that you house them, that they cannot stay in your place. See them sleeping up in the tree. If you have difficulty remembering the word "quarter," change its meaning for your visualization, and picture the tree also being covered with quarters.

4. The Fourth Amendment is the protection against search and seizure. Use your fourth peg (door) to protect you from the invasion of officers into your home. Picture yourself slamming the door in the faces of these men as you tell them that the Fourth

167

Amendment protects you, that they cannot legally enter your home to search or seize your property.

5. The Fifth Amendment is protection from self-incrimination. Picture peg five (hive), and see bees swarming around it. See yourself putting on special clothing to protect you from getting stung or from incriminating or testifying against yourself.

6. The Sixth Amendment is the right to a speedy trial. Picture the sixth peg (sticks) and see yourself picking up one of the sticks and shaking it at a judge, telling her to hurry and set the trial date for you. See yourself explaining to him that the Sixth Amendment requires that your trial be soon. Vividly visualize yourself running after the judge yelling the words, "Hurry, hurry!"

7. The Seventh Amendment is the right to a trial by jury. Visualize the peg for number seven, which is heaven. See a clear blue sky with white, fluffy clouds. See a jury of twelve members solemnly sitting in two straight rows across these clouds. Recognize that these people are members of the jury for your trial.

8. The Eighth Amendment, protection against cruel and unusual punishment, can easily be attached to peg eight (gate). Hear yourself being sentenced by a judge for a crime. The sentence is one that is both cruel and unusual: you will be slammed between the bars of a gate. The Eighth Amendment protects you against such an experience.

9. The Ninth Amendment is people's rights. See a group of people demanding the right to drink wine, peg number nine. Picture them raising the wine bottles to their mouths while chanting, "People's rights, people's rights."

10. The last amendment is states' rights. See the governor of your state standing on the steps of the state capitol building with a fat hen in his arms. Hear him giving a speech about the importance of

states' rights. See yourself wondering why the governor is holding the hen. Then smile when you see yourself remembering that the hen is your tenth peg.

Did these visualizations work for you? If some of them did not, create your own pictures, changing them to better match your background knowledge. Remember, personalized versions of mental pegs are usually more effective than book versions because the ones you make up incorporate your unique experiences.

Recognize too that once you have learned these mental pegs, they should stay with you for years. You may use them at any time to attach various sets of information you want to remember. The Peg system is merely a filing system for information. For instance, you may use peg words to memorize a list of artists for your humanities class or a group of theorists for your psychology class. The mental pegs remain the same through the years; only the information changes. It is possible to have many groups of information permanently stored in your memory all using the same peg filing system. When you want to retrieve the information, simply pull up your pegs and recall your visualizations.

Loci System

The **Loci system** is the oldest mnemonic technique known to man, dating back to 500 B.C. The word *loci*, which means "location" or "place," is an appropriate name because this system is based on recalling information associated with specific locations. Utilizing the principles of association and visualization, the Loci system aids organization, memorization, and retrieval of information.

The process is relatively simple. First, recall a familiar path that you use regularly such as the route you take to school or the path you follow between your classes. Some people use the floor plan of their home as their mental path. The path you choose can be almost anything as long as it is familiar to you. Once you have selected your path, choose specific points along the way as stopping places for

> The Loci system involves recalling a familiar path, selecting stopping places, and attaching information.

169

attaching information. Next, mentally review this path and the stopping places several times to firmly lock them in your mind. The following is an example of a loci path using the floor plan of a home. Notice that there are ten stopping places.

1. sidewalk	6. bedroom one
2. porch	7. bedroom two
3. front door	8. bathroom
4. living room	9. laundry room
5. kitchen	10. backdoor

Once the path is set in your mind, you can begin to attach the information you want to learn. Mentally draw pictures for each item you want to remember; then take an imaginary walk along the path and mentally place a piece of information at each stopping place. Using the location points above a path familiar to you, learn the following geological information. Associate the Loci points with the various sedimentary rocks. If you are familiar with any of these rocks, be sure to picture them in your mind. Having a mental image of the rocks will enhance your ability to learn the information.

Sedimentary Rocks

1. conglomerate	6. tufa
2. sandstone	7. oolite
3. siltstone	8. coquina
4. shale	9. travertine
5. limestone	10. dolomite

Now, visualize the following associations as you walk along this "mental path," and connect information to stopping places. Notice the numerical clues that are included to help you learn these rocks in order.

1. Your first stopping place is the sidewalk in front of your home. You are proud of this walk because it is both unusual and durable. Constructed of *conglomerate* rocks, your front walk has little pebbles and gravel embedded in the cement. You

chose this material for your sidewalk because you know that conglomerate rocks are the hardest of the sedimentary rocks.

2. Your second stopping place is the porch. You notice as you step up on the porch that there are *two* bags of sand on the stone floor (*sandstone*).

3. Your next stop is your front door. This door is a unique part of your home. Like your porch, the door is made of stone, but it has *three* panels made of silt. The silt contains fine particles of sand and clay. Your *siltstone* door is very unusual.

4. Your fourth stopping place is the living room. The floor in this room is extraordinarily beautiful. Made of genuine *shale*, the floor costs *four* thousand dollars.

5. You next walk into your kitchen. Some people may think your kitchen is rather strange because it is made of *limestone*. You note with pride, though, how much you like the looks of the limestone; then you laugh when you notice the *five* baskets of *limes* sitting on your counter. Aloud you say, "I hope these limes do not turn to *stone* before I can make them into pies."

6. Your sixth stop is the first bedroom, where your roommate Tu Fa (*tufa*) is sleeping amidst *six* bags of cookies and potato chips. Noticing how much weight he has put on, you decide that your roommate is too fat because all he has done for the last *six* days is sleep and eat.

7. You next walk across the hall to the second bedroom, where you notice that the afternoon sun is streaming through the *seven* window panes. Thinking how beautiful the light is, you exclaim, "Ooh light . . ." (*oolite*).

8. Your next stop is the bathroom across the hall. On the counter you notice *eight* items, including a coke, a key and a small letter *a*. You immediately say, "Great, now I will remember *coquina*!"

9. Your ninth stop is the laundry room. Just as you walk in the door, you remember that it is "travel time" (*travertine*); you need to leave for the airport at *nine* o'clock.

10. The last stop is your back door. As you open the door you remember that your friend *Dola might* (*dolomite*) bring her *ten* children for a visit.

Were you successful picturing the stopping places and seeing their connections to the sedimentary rocks? Could you create a similar visualization with information you need to learn for one of your classes? If you find that using mnemonics is valuable, you might want to read a book by Dr. Kenneth Higbee, *Your Memory: How It Works and How to Improve It*. Higbee discusses many additional memory techniques, including several more versions of peg systems. He also covers a phonetic mnemonic that is somewhat complex but quite versatile because it is much broader than either the Peg or Loci systems (Higbee, 1993).

METACOGNITIVE TRAINING ACTIVITY
Use Mnemonics
·꒳· MTA 5.5 ·꒳·

ᒲ DIRECTIONS:
Select one of the mnemonics discussed in this chapter.
Memorize at least 10 pieces of information for one of your classes.
Answer the following questions about your experience.

1. Which mnemonic(s) did you select?

2. What material did you try to learn?

3. Describe the mnemonic(s) you chose and how you connected it (them) to the material you wanted to learn.

4. Test yourself, or have someone test you to see if you remember the information. How well did you do?

5. Do you enjoy creating mnemonics? Why or why not?

6. Are these strategies helpful to you? Why or why not?

7. Self grade _____% and brief justification.

METACOGNITIVE TRAINING ACTIVITY
Rehearse
·೪· MTA 5.6 ·೪·

ʒ DIRECTIONS:

After completing a textbook chapter using all four stages in BICUM, begin to rehearse the information you have learned.

Continue rehearsing each week until you have taken a test on the material.

1. Schedule your first review session. When will it be, how long will it last, and where will you study? Mark this information on your calendar and record it here.

2. Conduct the first session, and record how long it actually took. Did you stay focused? Did you remember the material from your reductions? Does reviewing the information help you remember it more easily? Explain.

3. Plan regular weekly rehearsals using the metacognitive information you learned from your first session. Mark your study dates on your calendar, and write them here.

4. Continue rehearsing each week until you have a test on the material. Record the date of this test.

5. Take the test and record your score. Did rehearsing regularly help you perform better? Explain. What could you do to make your study sessions even more effective?

6. Self grade _____% and brief justification.

Rehearse

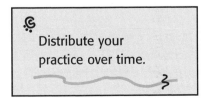

Distribute your practice over time.

The word *rehearse* is usually associated with plays. In order to be prepared to perform on stage in front of an audience, actors practice many hours. Day after day, for many weeks or months, they repeat their lines over and over again. With your studies, you should likewise rehearse or repeat what you want to remember and distribute your practice over time.

Begin early in the semester to learn information for your exams. After reading a section of text or taking notes on a class lecture, take a short break; then review or rehearse the information. Try to do this within twenty-four hours of hearing or reading the information. Wait a day or two, and review the information again. Read your next assignment and reduce it. Take a break; then review your previous assignment and look over the one you recently did.

Each week complete your new assignments by reading and reducing them; then review the information you have read in the past. Plan regular review sessions every week or two throughout the semester to rehearse your reduced forms. A few minutes of review on a consistent basis will help ensure that you do not forget what you have learned. Regular repetition helps hold information in your memory. If you follow this procedure, by the time midterms or finals arrive, you should be fully prepared and will probably not have to resort to cramming.

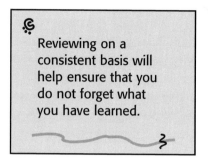

Reviewing on a consistent basis will help ensure that you do not forget what you have learned.

Summary

Learning and practicing memory techniques can make a decided difference in your success in college. This chapter contains many ideas for remembering information, including some of the most common and useful memory techniques used by college students. First, teaching someone is an especially powerful memory method because, for the most part, you will remember what you teach. Another memory technique, studying in groups, has the advantages of teaching someone and adds the power of group association. In groups, you teach each other, share information and ideas, and encourage each other during difficult times.

Third, recreating in writing is a helpful process for many students. Copying information or trying to reproduce it from memory while focusing on the meaning of what you are writing can lock ideas into your memory. An example of this is split-page testing. Fourth, for recall level learning, make study cards following the guidelines given in the chapter. Fifth, use mnemonics as memory aids, such as rhymes, acronyms, acrostics, mini stories, songs, and picture links. The Peg and Loci systems are also useful memory systems. They are fun to create and are very powerful. Sixth, rehearsing is the last memory technique mentioned in BICUM. This reminds you to schedule regular study sessions to go over the material you have learned.

Review Questions

1. What are three characteristics of short-term memory?

2. Explain how teaching someone can improve your chances of remembering material.

3. Why is studying in groups an effective strategy for many students but ineffective for others?

4. What is *blank page* testing? Name two retention methods that utilize this kind of testing.

5. Distinguish between recognition and recall level learning. Name two kinds of exams that usually require recall level learning.

6. Describe how to create effective study cards. Name one way you could use study cards in a course you are currently taking or in a class you plan to take in the future.

7. How is the Loci memory system different from the Peg system? Which system do you think you would be most likely to use? Why?

8. What are mnemonics, acronyms, and acrostics? Create an acronym to help you retain specific information for an exam. Include it in your answer with the information you plan to remember.

9. List the steps for creating acrostics. Use these steps to create an acrostic to remember information for a course exam. Include the acrostic and the course information in your response.

10. Describe the rehearse strategy and defend its use in education.

Metacognitive Insights

What have you learned about your memory? Which retention methods work best for you? Complete the following sentences. On the remaining lines add additional information that you have learned about yourself as you have read the chapter and completed the activities.

1. Teaching someone is _____

_____

_____

_____

2. Recreating in writing is _____

_____

_____

3. Using mnemonics can help me to _____

_____

_____

4. The best time each week for my study rehearsal is _____

_____

_____

ADDITIONAL INSIGHTS

_____

_____

_____

_____

_____

_____

_____

Create Your Own Bookmark

get **Ready**	**Read**	**Reduce**	**Retain**

PERSONALIZING **BICUM**

No great work is ever done in a hurry. To do anything great requires time, patience and perseverance. These things are done by degrees, "little by little." The greatest writers must begin with the alphabet, Shakespeare did not compose *Hamlet* in a day . . .

WILMONT BURTON

One of the greatest tasks college students can accomplish is to come to "know" themselves, not just to recognize their unique reading and learning styles, but to become aware of how they personally can best cope with school and with life. By using the metacognitive skills that you have developed throughout the textbook and practiced as you completed the MTAs, you have gradually increased your self-awareness and have begun the quest to know yourself.

Expanding your self-knowledge will require time, patience, and perseverance. You will need to continue practicing your metacognitive skills, just as Milton and Shakespeare continued to work on their masterpieces. As you do this, little by little you will discover bits of information about yourself. Knowing yourself is a significant accomplishment, one that is never quite complete because you are changing every moment. However, self-knowledge, incomplete as it may be, has the potential to dramatically impact your chances for success both in school and in life.

Overview: Four Reading Stages

Pause for a few moments and think about what you have learned as you have read, studied, and applied the strategies in this book. Have you noticed a definite improvement in your ability to handle college textbooks now that you know how to apply the four reading stages? If you are like most students, you are no longer overwhelmed with textbook reading assignments. You have begun to develop control over your own learning. In order to maintain the progress that you have made and to continue to improve your skills, you should use the techniques in the four stages of this study-reading program regularly and monitor your reading consistently.

Recognize that you do not have to memorize all of the strategies presented in order to successfully read textbooks. However, when reading is difficult to process and remember, you should use selected techniques from all four stages of the 4 R's: *Ready, Read, Reduce* and *Retain*. You can easily refer to the bookmark in the front of this text to refresh your memory on the various strategies in each stage. Keeping a copy of the bookmark in the textbook you are reading is a good idea. Remember that the bookmark is actually a brief outline of chapters two through five of this text, or the 4 R's for Remembering What You Read. If you forget how to use a strategy, just find the appropriate section to refresh your memory.

1. **Ready.** In the *Ready* stage you learned to prepare for your reading assignment. You learned these steps: Inventory SELF, Preview, Select or Create Questions, Set Study Times, and Place Control □'s. All of these strategies prepared you to successfully read textbooks.

2. **Read.** In the second step, *Read*, you were instructed to search for meaning. The following sentence was a reminder to you not to let words pass by your eyes without grasping meaning while attempting to read textbooks: *Reading is reading only when meaning is coming through.* Hopefully, now you catch yourself if your mind begins to wander.

   In the *Read* stage you also learned to read actively for meaning, fixing up any comprehension problems encountered along the way. You learned to place and use Control □'s to aid your concentration and to test your comprehension. If you successfully paraphrased what was read, you were ready to determine key information, mark and highlight your text, predict test questions, and then move forward to the next section of reading. If you could not repeat what was read, the five fix-up strategies were used to get back on track. In this stage you learned to continue the pattern of reading, testing and moving forward or fixing up problems until you completed your reading assignment. Once you could honestly say that the information was understood, then you were ready to go on to the next stage.

3. **Reduce.** In the *Reduce* stage you learned to simplify textbook material by creating a reduced form on separate paper. You were instructed to begin the reducing process by post-viewing the chapter and making sure you had answered all the questions you created before you began to read. Once you completed these strategies, you were to select a reduction technique. Four choices were given: making outlines, taking notes, writing summaries, and creating maps. Hopefully you tried all four methods and now have a good idea of which ones work well for you. Once you created a reduction form, you were directed to make sure it was complete enough that you could use it to study for exams without having to refer back to the text.

4. **Retain.** In the *Retain* stage, you learned several memory techniques designed to lock important information into your long-term memory. Teaching someone was the first one mentioned, followed by studying in groups, recreating in writing, and making study cards. You had probably used some of these techniques even before you read this text. Now that you recognize how powerful these strategies can be, you can use your metacognitive awareness to monitor and improve their effectiveness for you. Using mnemonics was the fifth memory technique mentioned. You learned that mnemonics are memory aids or memory tricks. They are actually based on the age-old principles of association and visualization. Examples of these creative memory aids are acronyms, acrostics and rhymes.

The last *Retain* strategy is significant: rehearse. It reminds you to set up regularly scheduled review sessions so that you don't forget the information you learned. Just as actors rehearse consistently over time, you must faithfully review what you learn. Your chances of remembering textbook material are much better if you rehearse and review regularly.

Make Some Modifications

As you know, this program presents a specific plan for successfully reading college texts. To understand and remember information from difficult college textbooks, you often may need to use strategies from most, if not all, of the stages. However, other times you may handle your assignments very successfully by using only a few parts of this plan. Remember that your study-reading needs to be personalized for each study task. It is not a strict process that must be followed exactly, but rather a flexible menu from which to select strategies or tools that fit your needs. Spend a few moments each time you study to decide what steps and strategies will be most helpful to you. If the text appears easy to understand and remember, you need only use a limited number of tools or methods from each stage. If the material seems more challenging, then you may need to incorporate combinations of techniques to insure retention. Here are some possible modifications that you may want to consider, depending upon your circumstances.

1. Stop at the end of the *Read* stage if the text appears easy to understand and remember.

   In this strategy, you get *Ready* to read by placing control boxes then stop at the end of the *Read* stage. Mark and highlight the important information at each stopping point. You may use your text as a study guide and not take the time to complete all of the strategies in the *Reduce* and *Retain* stages.

2. Make study cards if only parts of the chapter are challenging.

   Instead of creating one of the four comprehensive reduction forms suggested in BICUM (outlines, notes, summaries, or maps), reduce only part of your textbook chapter. Pull out the most important vocabulary terms or difficult concepts, and place them on study cards. This is a particularly good idea if you will be tested only on parts of a chapter.

3. Combine reduction forms if the material seems complicated.

You may use many possible combinations of reduction strategies. For example, you might combine notes and outlines. Simply write notes, but do them in an outline form. The Cornell format is useful because it has self-testing benefits. Just record the information in your notes section in an outline format instead of using the free-flowing words and phrases recommended with traditional note taking.

4. If the material is especially challenging, complete more than one reduction form.

You may decide that making only one reduction form is not sufficient. For example, you may find it helpful to make an outline and create a map. Completing these two reduction forms would engage both the left and the right sides of your brain in the thinking and recording processes, and therefore would be more powerful.

5. Formulate and answer questions as you read.

You learned to create questions before you read a chapter and then to answer them at the end. Instead of doing this, or in addition to it, try using the new ideas you discover to generate other questions as you read.

6. Study for more than 50 minutes if you have the ability to concentrate longer.

Although 50:10:50 is the recommended study-break-study ratio, try studying for an hour or an hour and a half. Longer study sessions may be especially productive when things are going well and you are actively involved. As you experience academic success, you may feel energized by the learning process. Use your metacognitive skills to determine when your interest starts to wane and you need to take breaks. Consciously notice whether you learn more with longer study sessions or whether you do better following the recommended study time.

7. If you remember the organizational layout of the chapter skip post viewing and answering questions.

Since you understand the key ideas and how they fit together, you may skip the techniques mentioned earlier. Go directly to reduction and retention strategies.

8. If you find it necessary to cram, use selected parts of the four reading stages.

Cramming is usually not a good idea, but if you get caught in a bind and need to cover several textbook chapters, you may have to do some last minute study-reading. You can learn to locate the important chapter information efficiently. Find out as much about the test as you can. Try to identify just what will be covered so you can concentrate your efforts on the material that will actually be on the test. For example, determine whether you should learn broad concepts or specific information, such as vocabulary terms, dates, names, and places. Once you decide what you need to know, spend the majority of your time memorizing the material in preparation for your test. Follow the steps below with each of the chapters you need to learn.

A. Preview the textbook chapter, reading the title, introduction, and summary.

B. Read the questions at the end of the chapter.

C. Read the headings and subheadings. Also, read a few lines after each of these items.

D. Notice any additional words in bold print, such as vocabulary and names of prominent persons. Define the words, and identify the contributions of each person listed if necessary.

E. Look for answers to the chapter questions.

F. Make study cards with this information, and spend your time memorizing it.

G. Do not try to learn everything in the chapter. Be satisfied with learning part of the chapter very well.

H. Take the test, and concentrate on the material you know. Use this information to make educated guesses on unfamiliar test questions.

Remember, cramming should not replace regular focused studying, but it can get you a passing grade in a pinch.

9. If you need to study when you are mentally weary or physically exhausted, read out loud to stay focused.

If you do not have time to take a nap or otherwise refresh yourself, try reading your textbook chapter aloud. If you are in a place where you can move about, combine vocalizing with pacing back and forth. Hearing your own voice and engaging in some physical movement can help keep you alert and can actually enhance your learning.

10. If you need variety, try combining two or more memory techniques.

Be creative—experiment with various combinations for aiding your memory. For example, try adding acronyms and/or acrostics on study cards, maps, or outlines. Draw visual clues in the margins of your textbook chapters to represent difficult or abstract concepts.

11. To fine tune, use control boxes to modify the technique.

Instead of simply placing a check (✓) in each box before continuing to read, analyze your comprehension level more closely by deciding how well you understand the information you have just read. If you still need more work to fully grasp the material, place a minus (−) in the box. If your understanding is ok, or good enough to pass a simple quiz or hold the information in your mind for just a short period of time, place a (✓) in the box. If you are certain that it is locked into your long-term memory, place a plus (+) in the box. Then mark or highlight the key information. Later, as you review for an exam, first work on the information that has a minus (−) in the box, then work on the checked (✓) information, and last, review the highlighted information followed by a plus (+).

As you consider what modifications to make in your reading plan, remember that the key to successful textbook reading is **to read for meaning.** Use whatever strategies are necessary to ensure that words do not pass by your eyes undetected and without meaning.

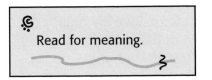

Read for meaning.

Create a Plan that Works for You

As you learned and practiced going through the four stages, did you discover preferences for particular strategies? For instance, did you find creating study cards helpful? Or, what about studying in groups? Do you know how beneficial discussing information with other students can be? You are now ready to use the answers to these questions and many others to create your own personalized study-reading program. With the metacognitive knowledge you have accumulated about your learning, you are prepared to design a study-reading plan that uniquely matches your particular learning style and course work.

As you make choices about what strategies to include in your personalized plan, it will be wise to use the strategy of placing control □'s. Remember that marking these stopping places and periodically testing your comprehension helps you stay on track and contributes to your reading success. If you discard this strategy, you may just read words without gaining the corresponding understanding. However, as you improve your reading skills, you should be able to place your control □'s farther apart. In other words, you will not need to stop as often to monitor your reading. Some students report that stopping to check their understanding becomes a habit and they no longer have to place □'s as reminders. Regular self-monitoring is of course the ideal.

Knowing many different learning steps and strategies frees you to choose options that match particular study needs, instead of being locked into one or two ways to learn. Be sure to include enough strategies in your plan to accommodate a variety of study needs.

Also, recognize that you do not have to alter BICUM to make it a part of your personal plan. You can choose to follow this study-reading program exactly. BICUM stages and strategies have proven useful to thousands of students. There is enough variety in the program to meet most students' needs. Just keep your mind open for new ideas and possible changes. And, if you do decide to alter the plan, periodically refer back to the BICUM bookmark or to this textbook to make certain that you have not left out a strategy that might be helpful to you. Since you are changing every day, and since new and improved study techniques are being introduced continuously, your study-reading must be an ongoing, ever-changing process. Use your metacognitive skills to continuously build and improve your personalized program.

Your Personalized Study Plan

Refer to the Metacognitive Insights pages to help you create your personalized BICUM plan.

Use the page entitled My Personalized BICUM Plan (page 188) to create your individual study-reading plan. You may wish to make several photocopies of this page before you fill in your plan. That way you will have blank copies when you want to make revisions later.

Refer to the Metacognitive Insights worksheets that you completed at the end of each chapter. The information you recorded as you were learning and practicing each stage will now remind you which strategies work best for you. Use these pages as guidelines to fill in the blank lines in your personalized plan. For example, if you recorded a metacognitive insight that you learn best when you write information, be sure to include a strategy that incorporates writing in your *Retain* category. Or, if you wrote that you stay focused better when you create questions before reading, be sure to list Make Questions as a strategy in the *Ready* stage. Remember, you can leave out strategies that you did not find especially helpful.

The information you learned from completing the MTAs in each chapter will help you recall the strategies that best meet your learning needs. In addition, you may wish to include some of the modifications mentioned earlier in this chapter and list any useful strategies that you have discovered on your own or learned from other sources.

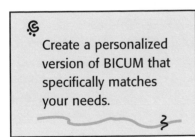

Create a personalized version of BICUM that specifically matches your needs.

Your goal in creating a personalized version of BICUM is to assemble a group of reading and learning strategies that specifically match your needs. Start with the *Ready* stage and list all of the strategies you use to prepare to read textbook assignments. Next, move to the *Read* stage and write strategies that help you read actively and understand material in textbooks. Be sure to include the fix-up strategies that help you efficiently get back on track when your comprehension breaks down.

Now, fill in the *Reduce* stage by writing the techniques that help you "pull out" and record the important parts of textbook chapters. Decide which of the four reduction methods most often meets your needs with various kinds of course material. But remember that most students find that one of these reductions is sufficient for any particular chapter or section of text unless they have discovered that additional organizing and writing practice is necessary.

Personalized BICUM Plan

Ready   **Read**

_____   _____

_____   _____

_____   _____

_____   _____

_____   _____

_____   _____

_____   _____

_____   _____

Reduce   **Retain**

_____   _____

_____   _____

_____   _____

_____   _____

_____   _____

_____   _____

FIGURE 6.1 PERSONALIZED BICUM PLAN

Only include those activities that really help you remember information.

Finally move to the *Retain* stage. List the memory techniques you use to lock important information in your mind. Be sure to add additional memory strategies that you have learned from other sources. Only include those activities that really help you remember information.

Be sure to plan a regular time to review or rehearse the information you need to learn. If most people do not regularly review information, they forget or have great difficulty retrieving material when the need arises.

The selections you make as you create your personalized BICUM program do not have to stay the same. In fact, you may even choose to make modifications the next time you study. However, the plan you create now can serve as a guide as you continue to take conscious control of your college reading. Regularly use your metacognitive skills to appraise the effectiveness of using the specific steps and techniques that you included in your personalized plan. Then make adjustments as your study needs change.

Test-Taking Tips: Prove that You Remember

In college, not only is it necessary to read and understand difficult textbooks, but you also have to prove to your instructors that you remember the information you read. This proof is often required in the form of written exams. Unfortunately, many students are frightened by tests, and this anxiety interferes with their performance.

Test Anxiety

Test anxiety is quite common and is experienced by almost all students to some degree. However, worrying about taking tests can result in a number of problems. First, test anxiety is usually not task-focused. For example, it often involves negative self-focused thoughts that can interfere with concentration and the ability to accurately record answers. Second, inability to accurately record information translates into poor test performance, which reinforces the negative self-thoughts that lead to poor test performance. The result is a vicious cycle of negative thoughts leading to poor performance, and poor performance leading to negative thoughts. Third, over time students may give up hope and decide to drop out of school rather than face further failure.

A simple technique that many students find useful to control negative thoughts is "thought stopping." This method involves monitoring your thoughts, mentally telling yourself "stop!" whenever negative ideas come into your mind, then replacing them with positive thoughts. Practicing this technique before, during, and after testing can help decrease negative thinking.

Actually the best cure for test anxiety is wise preparation. If you have actively followed the 4 R's in BICUM, you have already completed many activities that will help your performance on tests. Your wise preparation should serve you well in testing situations.

Following are some additional test-taking tips that you may want to consider completing before, during, and after taking tests to further improve your scores.

Before the Test

1. Prepare from the start.

    Buy your textbook early and preview or read each chapter before your teacher discusses the information in class. Having some advanced knowledge of the material to be covered will equip your mind to more readily learn about the subject.

2. Attend class regularly. Be on time, and do not leave early.

    There is a direct correlation between attendance and grades on exams. Students who never miss class are much more likely to earn higher test scores than students who only attend intermittently. Essential explanations and assignments are often given as class begins and ends.

3. Take notes.

    Be attentive during the lectures. Write down important information. Do not try to record everything that your instructor says. Instead, write only key ideas, usually in phrases instead of sentences. The note-taking guidelines that you learned in chapter 5, such as using abbreviations, also apply to class lectures.

4. Sit in the "Terrific T" of the classroom.

The seats across the front and the seats down the middle of the classroom are more conducive to active class involvement. If you sit in this area, you are more likely to stay focused and pick up the important information that will be covered on tests.

5. Ask questions in class.

Asking questions helps you become personally involved in the lecture. As a result, you are more likely to stay interested in the material and remember the information.

6. Complete all assignments on time.

Read your text chapter by chapter, reducing each one as you go. Regularly review the material that you have previously covered and keep up to date with additional assignments. Do not allow yourself to get behind. Having to catch up at the same time that you are trying to complete current assignments can be disastrous.

7. Call classmates for assistance.

If you are ill and cannot attend class, check with a classmate so you can return prepared. If you miss information as you take notes, classmates may be able to help you fill in the gaps. Conferring with them over confusing points in the text or lectures, checking to make sure you have recorded assignments correctly, or confirming test dates can prevent some possible frustrations later.

8. Designate a study area and time.

Studying in a regular place and at set times will help you be a more efficient learner and aid in test preparation.

9. Find out what the test will cover.

Except for pop quizzes, instructors will likely tell you in advance what will be on the test. If you are uncertain, be sure to ask for clarification. Also, find out what percentage of the test will come from class notes and what percentage will result from textbook reading.

10.   Find out the type of test.

Knowing whether an exam will be multiple choice, true/false, or essay can also help you study more efficiently. For example, essay tests demand recall level learning. If this is the type of test you will be taking, plan to study more thoroughly. Prepare by writing answers to practice essay questions.

11.   Predict possible test questions.

Few teachers give out exact exam questions, but many teachers give strong hints as to what information will be included on exams. Occasionally instructors will have copies of old tests available upon request. If you are conscientious, you can learn to "read" your instructors and anticipate test questions. For instance, they might say, "This is important to remember," or "This would make a good test question." Instructors might also write important information on the board or print it on overheads. Any time teachers emphasize ideas, be aware that the information may appear on a test. Learn to watch for these hints; record and highlight possible test questions in your notes and directly in your text. This is an appropriate place to mark with a **T** to signal text questions, as suggested in chapter 3.

12.   Make up, take, and correct practice tests.

Dr. Ruel A. Allred, a nationally known reading expert, believes that a great deal of learning can take place during the testing process. He believes that this is especially true if students correct their own tests and receive prompt and correct feedback. Also, many educators suggest that taking practice exams can help students reduce their test anxiety.

You can take the advice from these experts and begin to learn from self-testing and reduce your fear of taking tests. Review the hints you noticed from your teachers on possible exam questions. Look over the chapter questions in your textbook and your reduced forms. Consider all this information as you construct a practice test.

Wait a day or so and take the test. Be sure to write the answers to your questions, as you will probably have to write the answers on your test. Few teachers give oral exams. It is possible to be able to answer questions vocally, then forget the information when you must write it. Make your practice test as similar to the actual exam as possible so you will not have this problem. Very soon after you finish your practice test, correct it. Notice what you missed and why; then learn that material also.

13. Prepare yourself physically.

Do not stay up all night studying. Get a good night's sleep before your test so you can think clearly. Also, eat a nutritious breakfast.

14. Review your notes just before going to bed and soon after you awake.

Take advantage of your subconscious mind. Look over your notes before going to bed so your mind can process the material while you are sleeping. Then, when you wake up, review your notes again to increase your chances of success on your test.

During the Test

1. Arrive a few minutes early.

Plan to arrive a few minutes before the test is scheduled to begin. That way if something unexpected occurs you may at least be on time. Rushing in late gets you off on the wrong foot and can interfere with your concentration. If you give yourself a few spare moments, you can collect your thoughts and mentally prepare yourself to succeed.

2. Use a two-minute spill.

Before looking at the test, jot down on a piece of scratch paper everything you want to remember. (You may need to ask in advance for permission to use scratch paper so you will not be accused of cheating.) Record the acronyms you learned, the words that they are connected to, and the lists of ideas you memorized. Writing this information down can give you a sense of security and decrease your test anxiety. Even if you forget other information, you can be assured that the ideas you wrote in your two-minute spill are safe. Having a written copy of some important information can be comforting.

3.　Think positively. Tell yourself that you can do well.

Do not allow yourself to dwell on negative ideas or fears. A well-known writer, James Allen, once said, "As a man thinketh, so is he." If his idea were to be applied to test taking, it might read, "As a student thinketh he/she will do on an exam, so will he/she do." The power of the mind to control actions is sometimes called self-fulfilling prophecy. Whether you think you can or think you can't, you are right. If you have prepared wisely, you can and definitely should confidently say to yourself, " I will do well on this test."

4.　Preview the test before you start.

Quickly look over your test. Count the pages. Notice the number of questions and what types of questions are included. Are there point values attached to the questions? If so, notice which ones are worth the most.

5.　Plan your time.

If you have limited time in which to complete the test, be careful to plan your time wisely. Assign a specific number of minutes to spend on each question. Consider the point values of each one. Spend more time on the ones that are worth the most. Include five minutes to look over your test when you finish.

6.　Read carefully.

Students often misread or overlook test directions. As a result, they lose points. Also, many students miss questions because they do not read them correctly or do not follow the directions precisely. For example, if there are three parts to a question, be sure to answer all three parts. Many students inadvertently answer only a portion of some questions. As a consequence, they miss points, sometimes on information they know very well. Do not let simple reading errors lower your test scores.

7.　Ask for clarification on poorly worded questions.

If you do not understand a question, ask your instructor. If this is not possible, write your concerns and reasoning on a piece of paper, or in the margins on the test. If you used an additional page, attach it to the test when you turn it in. Instructors will often give credit for alternate answers if your reasoning is valid.

8. Go through the test three times.

The first time, answer all the questions you are sure about. This builds confidence and reduces test anxiety. The second time, answer the harder questions; the third time check your work for accuracy and review the answers that you were unsure of. Be cautious about changing answers. Often your first impression is the right choice.

9. Pick up hints for answers throughout the test.

Use the information in other questions to answer the questions that puzzle you. If you come to a question that stumps you, leave it blank and work through the rest of the test. Many times you will find some of the information you forgot given in another question. Using this information can save you points that you otherwise might have lost.

10. Answer every question.

Unless you are penalized for incorrect responses, never leave a question blank. Guessing can often add a few additional points to your score.

11. Follow specific tips for taking true/false tests.

A. Answer the questions as quickly as possible, and don't waste time looking for hidden meanings.

B. All of the information in a question must be true for the whole question to be true.

C. If questions are long and complicated, they are more likely to be false. Because there are many parts included in these sentences, it is easy to overlook a minor but nevertheless significant untrue word or phrase. Evaluate these sentences very carefully.

D. Watch for absolute words, such as "invariably," "never," "always," "all." Generally the questions that contain absolute words are false.

E. Assume that a question is true unless you can determine what makes it false. It must be true without exception. Statements tend to be false when they state a reason. They tend to give an incorrect reason or they don't give all the possible reasons.

F. If a test item contains two statements, both must be true for the item to be true.

G. Watch out for "not" and other negative words. These change answers to the opposite of what you expect. Negative words are very easy to overlook. Consciously look for them so you won't lose points.

12. Follow specific tips for taking multiple choice tests.

A. Eliminate impossible, illogical or irrelevant answers. If you narrow down the possibilities to choose from, you will have a greater chance of getting the answers right.

B. Read all the options before answering questions. Sometimes the answer that first appears correct is not as good as another one of the options. Often your task is to select the "best answer." More than one answer may be correct, but one will be better than the others.

C. If you narrow down the answer to two similar-looking phrases, decide how the two differ and how the differences make one correct and the other wrong.

D. As with true/false tests, watch out for negative words. You might try circling them so they will stand out and you can take them into consideration when you answer.

E. Absolute words (always, never, all, etc.) are just as important to notice in multiple choice questions as they are in true/false questions. Usually questions that contain these words are false. Few situations are 100% one way or the other.

F. Answers with qualifying words such as "often," "usually," and "generally," are often correct.

G. If you have studied thoroughly and are well prepared to take the test, you can usually assume that multiple choice options containing unfamiliar words, sentences and phrases are incorrect.

H. The longest option is often the correct option, particularly if the test was created by your instructor. In creating the test, your teacher likely created the correct option first, making sure it included all the necessary information to make it correct. Then he/she constructed the alternate answers and probably didn't take as much time to create them or found it difficult to create good distractors. Therefore, they might be shorter and less comprehensive. (This will probably not work on professionally constructed tests because they have been reviewed several times, and hints like this would likely have been eliminated.)

I. The correct answer will agree grammatically with the stem (beginning part of the question). Sometimes incorrect answers do not match. Again, the correct option is often created first, and great care is taken to eliminate any confusion in the answer. The other options might not have been as carefully constructed, so they might not agree grammatically. (Don't look for this hint in professionally constructed tests. Flaws like this would likely have been found and corrected.)

13. Follow specific tips for taking essay tests.

A. Read through the entire test before beginning to answer any of the questions. As you do this, jot down thoughts in the margins that you want to include in your answers.

B. If you are being timed, it is especially important in essay tests to plan how long you can afford to spend on each question. Also, allow a few minutes to look over your answers. Filling in words you left out or cleaning up confusing thoughts can add valuable points.

C. Mark the important direction words that tell you what to do: "compare," "describe," "list," "define," and so on. Be sure you follow them precisely.

D. Often essay questions have multiple parts. Number each one so that you remember to answer *all* of them.

E. If time permits, briefly outline your answers before you begin to write. Having a plan to follow will help you state your information more clearly and avoid rambling.

F. Use the first sentence as your main idea. Do not include an introduction. Creative writing is not appropriate for answering essay questions. You do not have to introduce your instructor to the topic; just clearly state what you have to say.

G. Follow the main idea with clear supports, using numbers or transition words to indicate these points (first, second, another reason is, also, etc.).

H. End your essay with a summary statement that ties your ideas together. This can be as simple as restating the main idea.

I. If you run short of time, quickly outline answers to the questions that remain. List the information without worrying about writing complete sentences. You will likely receive at least partial credit.

After the Test

1. Look up any material on the test.

Go to your text or notes and find the answers to the questions you were unsure of on the test. Once you find the material, recall your reasoning during the test. Ask yourself why you answered the questions the way you did. You can learn a lot about your testing behavior when you answer these metacognitive questions.

2. Ask to see a copy of the test. Find out which questions you missed and why you missed them.

If your instructor hands back the tests and goes over the answers with you, pay careful attention. For each question you missed, find out precisely why you marked it incorrectly. Check to see if any of the following questions explain your mistakes.

A. Did you misread the questions?

B. Did you overlook negative words or absolute words?

C. Did you know the material but mistakenly mark the wrong answers? (This is a common mistake.)

D. Did you fail to study the material you missed? If so, find out the sources of this information: lectures, notes, text, etc. Maybe you were simply unaware of material for which you were held responsible.

E. Did you read more into questions than was really there? It is possible to over-analyze a question and unknowingly include information that is not actually required to answer correctly.

F. Did you change answers and not erase completely? Scantron checkers are very sensitive to smudges and stray marks.

If your instructors do not normally hand back tests, be assertive and politely ask to spend time in their offices reviewing the exams. Most instructors are very willing to accommodate sincere students.

3. Positively reinforce yourself on the questions you answered correctly.

Notice how much of the test you answered correctly, and tell yourself that you did a good job. Even a sixty percent on a test means that you got more than half of the questions right. If you consciously praise yourself, you are less likely to have negative thoughts enter your mind when you take future tests. Remember that negative thinking can interfere with your concentration and cause low test performance. Make a point to compliment and/or reward yourself for your successes (however small they may be).

4. If you did poorly, see if you can retake the test.

If your instructor offers retakes, be sure to take advantage of them. Some teachers give repeat tests that are averaged with the initial tests. Be sure you are aware of your options.

5. Decide what you can do differently to prepare better for the next test.

Take all the information you have accumulated from the above questions, and make a plan of how to prepare for your next test. Remember that testing can be a learning experience. You can make this happen for you if you use your metacognitive skills to learn from your mistakes. For example, if you noticed that you missed several questions from your notes, plan to review your notes more carefully next time. Or if you noticed you overlooked the word "not" and recorded the opposite answer, you can plan to circle this word on succeeding tests. The information you have gained about yourself as a test taker can help you improve in future performance.

Summary

Coming to know yourself is an ongoing process, one that can help you succeed in school and in life. The BICUM study-reading program directs you to learn and use metacognitive skills to gain knowledge about yourself. This chapter overviews BICUM, quickly reviewing the four stages and their strategies. Several possible modifications are presented, and you are encouraged to create your own personal version of study-reading.

For many students, taking tests is frightening. Test anxiety is experienced by almost every student. Thought stopping is a simple technique that may help, but the best prevention for test anxiety is preparation. Learning to take control of your reading helps you prepare adequately for tests. Using additional test taking tips before, during, and after tests will likely increase your test scores.

Review Questions

1. After reading this textbook, identify four of your favorite study-reading techniques, one from each of the 4 R's, and tell briefly why you chose each one.

2. Is it necessary to strictly follow every step and strategy in BICUM each time you study-read? Explain.

3. Suggest three modifications you might make when using the BICUM system in your future study. Describe the benefits of making these changes.

4. Identify two test taking tips you might use *before* taking a test, and tell why you would use them.

5. What techniques from BICUM could you use if you must cram for a test?

6. Assess your typical level of anxiety when you take tests and state what it is. Discuss ways to reduce your present level of test anxiety or help someone else reduce theirs.

7. Support the idea that using the "Terrific T" can increase student effectiveness.

8. Do you agree or disagree with the statement by Dr. Allred that a great deal of learning takes place during the testing process? Defend your answer.

9. Review the test-taking tips listed in this chapter for use *during* testing. Select the three you consider the most useful and tell why.

10. What could you say to a classmate to convince him/her to use test taking tips *after* completing an exam?

Metacognitive Insights

What have you learned about your test-taking abilities?
Complete the following sentences. On the remaining lines add
additional information that you have learned about yourself as
you have read the chapter and completed the activities.

1. I need to start focused preparation _____ days before a test so that _____

   _____

   _____

2. Taking tests makes me feel _____

   _____

   _____

3. I do best when I prepare for a test by _____

   _____

   _____

ADDITIONAL INSIGHTS

_____

_____

_____

_____

_____

_____

_____

_____

_____

_____

APPENDIX A: PRACTICE PARAGRAPHS

1. For many people, Ludwig van Beethoven (1770–1827) represents the highest level of musical genius. He opened new realms of musical expression and profoundly influenced composers throughout the nineteenth century. By the age of eleven, he was serving as assistant to the court organist, and at age twelve he had several compositions published. When he was sixteen, he played for Mozart, who reportedly said, "Keep your eyes on him; some day he will give the world something to talk about."

Music: An Appreciation, Roger Kamien

2. With Lee's army gone, remaining resistance throughout the Confederacy collapsed within a matter of weeks. Visiting the captured city of Richmond on April 4, Lincoln was enthusiastically greeted by the black population. He looked "pale, haggard, utterly worn out," noted one observer. The lines in his face showed how much the war had aged him in only four years. Often his friends had counseled rest, but Lincoln had observed that "the tired part of me is inside and out of reach." The burden, he confessed, was almost too much to bear.

Nation of Nations, James W. Davidson

3. Note taking gives you a record of the speaker's most important points. Unless you have superhuman powers of memory, there is no way you can remember all of a speaker's key ideas without taking notes. Note taking sharpens and strengthens your ability to listen analytically. When you take notes, you force your mind to scan a speech like radar, looking for main points and evidence. Taking notes whenever you listen to a lecture has these and other benefits. Note taking is a good way to keep your attention on the speaker and not let your mind wander. This is why I recommend taking notes on all speeches—not just on important lectures at school.

Public Speaking, Hamilton Gregory

4. In 1938, 1 in 5 Americans approved "of a married woman holding a job in business or industry if her husband is able to support her." By 1993, 86 percent approved (Newport,1993)—although nearly 2 in 3 still think that for children the "ideal family situation" is "father has a job and mother stays home and cares for the children" (Gallup, 1990). In 1967, 57 percent of first-year American collegians agreed that "the activities of married women are best confined to the home and family." In 1994, 25 percent agreed (Austin & others, 1987,1994). In the last half-century—a thin slice of our long history—gender roles have changed dramatically.

Social Psychology, David G. Myers

5. Politically, the war dramatically changed the balance of power. The South lost its substantial influence, as did the Democratic party, while the Republicans emerged in a dominant position. The Union's military victory signaled the triumph of nationalism. The war destroyed the idea that the Union was a voluntary confederacy of sovereign states, which theorists like John C. Calhoun had argued, and that the states had the right to secede. In an important symbolic change, Americans now spoke of the United States in the singular rather than the plural.

Nation of Nations, James W. Davidson

6. People in western society hold particularly well-defined stereotypes about men and women, and those stereotypes prevail regardless of age, economic status, and social and educational background. Men are more apt to be viewed as having traits involving competence, such as independence, objectivity, and competitive-expressiveness. In contrast, women tend to be seen as having traits involving warmth and expressiveness, such as gentleness and awareness of others' feelings. Because our society traditionally holds competence in higher esteem than warmth and expressiveness, the perceived differences between men and women are biased in favor of men.

Understanding Psychology, Robert S. Feldman

7. If you are like most people, you have indulged in fake listening many times. You go to history class, sit in the third row, and look squarely at the instructor as she speaks. But your mind is far away, floating in the clouds of a pleasant daydream. Occasionally you come back to earth: the instructor writes an important term on the chalkboard, and you dutifully copy it in your notebook. Every once in a while the instructor makes a witty remark, causing others in the class to laugh. You smile politely, pretending that you have heard the remark and found it mildly humorous. You have a vague sense of guilt that you are not paying close attention, but you tell yourself that any material you miss can be picked up from a friend's notes. Besides, the instructor is talking about road construction in ancient Rome and nothing could be more boring. So, back you go into your private little world.

Public Speaking, Hamilton Gregory

8. Franz Liszt (1811–1886) was handsome, magnetic, irresistible to women, an incredible showman, and a pacesetter in musical history. During the 1840s, he performed superhuman feats at the piano, overwhelming the European public and impressing musicians as much as concert goers. Chopin wished that he could play his own piano etudes the way Liszt did. Schumann wrote that Liszt "enmeshed every member of the audience with his art and did with them as he willed." Brahms later said, "Whoever has not heard Liszt cannot speak of piano playing."

Music: An Appreciation, Roger Kamien

9. At first radio was seen as a civilizing force. "The air is your theater, your college, your newspaper, your library," exalted one ad in 1924. But with the growing number of sets came commercial broadcasting, catering to more common tastes. Almost the entire nation listened to "Amos 'n' Andy," a comedy about black Americans created by two white vaudevillians in 1929. At night families gathered around the radio instead of the hearth, listening to a concert, perhaps, rather than going out to hear music. Ticket sales at vaudeville theaters collapsed. The aged, the sick, and the isolated, moreover, could be "at home but never alone," as one radio ad declared. Linked by nothing but airwaves, Americans were finding themselves part of a vast new community of listeners.

Nation of Nations, James W. Davidson

10. Retrieval cues guide people through the information stored in long-term memory in much the same way as the cards in a card catalog guide people through a library. They are particularly important when we are making an effort to recall information, as opposed to our being asked to recognize material stored in memory. In recall, a specific piece of information must be retrieved, such as that needed to answer a fill-in-the-blank question or write an essay on a test. In contrast, recognition occurs when people are presented with a stimulus and asked whether they have been exposed to it previously, or are asked to identify it from a list of alternatives.

Understanding Psychology, Robert S. Feldman

11. Encoding refers to the process by which information is initially recorded in a form usable to memory. Memory specialists speak of storage as the maintenance of material saved in the memory system. If the material is not stored adequately, it cannot be recalled later. Memory also depends on one last process: retrieval. In retrieval, material in memory storage is located, brought into awareness, and utilized. Psychologists consider memory as the process by which we encode, store, and retrieve information. Each of the three parts of this definition—encoding, storage, and retrieval—represents a different process, which you can think of as analogous to a computer's keyboard (encoding), disk (storage), and screen (retrieval). And only if all three processes have operated will you experience success and be able to recall the information you are trying to remember.

Understanding Psychology, Robert S. Feldman

APPENDIX B:
PATTERNS OF ORGANIZATION

The patterns of organization are described in the chart below. To understand the patterns it may be helpful to memorize these definitions and a few clue or signal words for each pattern. Personalizing the information from the chart by putting the definition into your own words and by memorizing a few of the clue words that make the most sense to you from each pattern will help you learn them.

Name of Pattern	Definition	Examples of Clue Words in Text	
Listing	Supporting details are in a list format, which means they may appear in any order.	one, first, second, also, another, in addition, finally, last of all	
Sequence	The major details must be arranged in a particular order, such as in steps, processes, and procedures.	before, during, next, when, often, now, then, after, first, second, also (*Note:* Some of these key words also appear in the listing pattern.)	
Comparison/Contrast	Two or more concepts or things are being examined for their similarities or differences.	**Comparison** like, just as, likewise, similarly	**Contrast** but, however, in contrast, even though, instead
Cause/Effect	The reasons that things happen and their results are presented. (*Note:* the result will often be presented first)	because, reason, since, so, thus, if . . . then, as a result, therefore	
Illustration	One or more examples or explanations are given to develop an understanding of a concept.	for instance, to illustrate, such as, for example, once, including	

Listing Pattern

One of the most common organizational techniques is *listing*. This pattern is often used when authors want to add information to make the main idea more understandable. In this pattern the major details are not arranged in any particular order. Understanding how the major details relate to the main idea is a key to understanding what pattern the author is using. That is one reason why being able to determine main ideas and major supporting details is so important. Seeing patterns in writing helps readers gain a deeper understanding of how sentences and paragraphs work together to convey meaning.

Part of the comprehension process also involves becoming aware of how clue or signal words can sometimes help indicate or predict the authors pattern of organization. Below is one of the paragraphs, previously used in chapter 3, to illustrate this idea. Looking at this paragraph while you keep the listing pattern in mind will take you to a higher level of comprehension.

The American Revolution was an accelerated evolution rather than outright revolution in the sense of a radical or total change. It did not suddenly and violently overturn the entire political and social framework, as later occurred in the French and Russian revolutions. During the conflict itself people went on working and praying, marrying and playing. Most of them were not seriously disturbed by the actual fighting, and many of the more isolated communities scarcely knew that a war was going on.

(Revised) *The American Pageant,* Bailey and Kennedy

Topic: The American Revolution was not an outright revolution.

Main idea: The American Revolution was not a revolution in the sense of a radical or total change.

Major details: (1) It did not suddenly and violently overturn the entire political and social framework. (2) People went on working, praying, marrying, and playing. (3) Most people were not seriously disturbed by the actual fighting. (4) Many of the more isolated communities scarcely knew that a war was going on.

As you can see, the major supporting details add information to make the main idea statement understandable. After reading these supports, it is easy to understand why the author believed that the American Revolution did not involve radical or total change.

Note that the supporting details could have been stated in a different order and would still support the main idea in an equally efficient manner.

Sequence Pattern

Unlike listing, *sequence* has the major supporting details organized in a way that they cannot be rearranged without changing the meaning. Some examples of this pattern would include paragraphs or passages that discuss such things as historical events, steps that need to be followed in order, procedures, and processes. Notice the chronological order of the following passage, detailing a few musical accomplishments of Beethoven.

> For many people, Ludwig van Beethoven (1770–1827) represents the highest level of musical genius. He opened new realms of musical expression and profoundly influenced composers throughout the nineteenth century. By the age of eleven, he was serving as assistant to the court organist, and at age twelve he had several compositions published. When he was sixteen, he played for Mozart, who reportedly said, "Keep your eyes on him; some day he will give the world something to talk about."
>
> *Music: An Appreciation*, Roger Kamien

Notice the references to the ages at which Beethoven rose to levels of musical expression. Using references to time or dates is typical of the sequence pattern. As you become aware of this pattern, you will begin to notice its use in many kinds of reading such as science, math, and computer science.

Comparison/Contrast

The third pattern on the chart is the comparison/ contrast pattern in which two or more things are being examined for their similarities or differences. We often use the term "comparison" in colloquial speech when we are analyzing both the similarities and the differences between at least two things. This use of comparison is fine in casual conversation, but the term takes on a slightly different meaning when used in the academic task of determining authors' patterns of organization. During this scholastic activity comparison means to draw connections between ideas or things that are *similar*, while "contrast" is the expression that is used when examining *differences*. Read this paragraph to determine what two things are being compared, contrasted, or both.

> People in western society hold particularly well-defined stereotypes about men and women, and those stereotypes prevail regardless of age, economic status, and social and educational background. Men are more apt to be viewed as having traits involving competence, such as independence, objectivity, and competitive-expressiveness. *In contrast*, women tend to be seen as having traits involving warmth and expressiveness, such as gentleness and awareness of others' feelings. Because our society traditionally holds competence in higher esteem than warmth and expressiveness, the perceived differences between men and women are biased in favor of men. [Emphasis added]
>
> *Understanding Psychology*, Robert S. Feldman

Here the distinction is made between stereotypes of men and women in western culture and the roles that are valued more in society. The paragraph is straightforward in discussing the contrasting views regarding men and women, although the only discussion of similarities is about the commonly held stereotypes of both. Notice the clue words, *in contrast*, that the author uses to signal the discussion of differences in the stereotypes held about men and women by western society.

Cause/Effect

The following paragraph is a good example of the fourth pattern, *cause and effect*. It presents the reasons why things happen and the results. As you read the paragraph, try to determine what cause or reason and effect or result are presented.

> In the seventeenth century, sailors at sea frequently suffered from muscle weakness and unexplained bleeding. Often this disease proved fatal until it was discovered that sailors who ate oranges or lemons either did not get sick or else suffered from a milder form of the disease. As a result, British navy officials passed a law requiring that every ship provide oranges and lemons for the crew. By accident, the navy had discovered that these citrus fruits which contained vitamin C prevented the disease we now know as scurvy.
>
> *Reading for Success*, Laraine E. Flemming

The above paragraph describes the symptoms such as muscle weakness, unexplained bleeding, and sometimes death that resulted from a lack of vitamin C in the diet of seventeenth century British sailors. Notice that these symptoms were the effects, and the cause of the disease was not eating citrus fruits containing vitamin C. It is important to realize that while in real life the cause(s) always occurs first, frequently when events are reported, the effect(s) are often mentioned first to get the readers' attention. For example, think of headlines in most newspapers or reports of scientific studies. The effect(s) are usually given first, followed by detailed explanations of the cause(s). It is also useful to realize that one cause, such as an earthquake, can have a number of effects, and vice versa.

Illustration Pattern

The *illustration* pattern is one in which the author makes a point, then supports it by giving one or more examples or explanations to help readers develop an understanding of the information. The illustration pattern will often contain definitions followed by one or more examples to clarify new concepts for the reader. One of the main goals in every content area text, such as psychology, is to teach the terminology that is essential for an intelligent discussion of each discipline. An example of this pattern is given in the paragraph that follows, taken from the article about Piaget's Theory in chapter 3. Notice how certain terms are defined, then examples are given to illuminate or illustrate what the author is trying to convey about this stage of children's cognitive development.

> **Concrete Operations Stage: Seven to Twelve Years.** The beginning of this stage is marked by mastery of the principle of conservation. During this stage, children develop the ability to think in a more logical manner, and they begin to overcome some of the egocentric characteristics of the preoperational period. Also, they are able to understand the principle of *reversibility*, the idea that some changes can be undone by reversing an earlier action. For instance, they understand that a ball of clay may be shaped into a coil and then be reshaped into a ball again.

Patterns of organization don't always need to be consciously identified. Once you become proficient at recognizing them, you will be able to anticipate the author's train of thought and understand the key points. This skill will not only help in reading more effectively but will also enhance your writing ability.

REFERENCES

Anderson, R. (1994). Role of the reader's schema in comprehension, learning, and memory. In R. B. Ruddell, M. R. Ruddell, & H. Singer (Eds.), *Theoretical models and processes of reading* (pp. 469–482). Newark, DE: International Reading Association.

Atkinson, R. C., & Schiffrin, R. M. (1968). Human memory: A proposed system and its control processes. In K. W. Spence (Ed.), *The psychology of learning and motivation: Advances in research and theory*, 2nd ed. (pp. 89–195). New York: Academic Press.

Bailey, T. A., Kennedy, D. M., & Cohen, L. (1998). *The American Pageant*, 11th ed. Boston: Houghton Mifflin.

Bandura, A. (1986). *Social foundations of thought and action: A social cognitive theory.* Englewood, NJ: Prentice-Hall.

Baron, R. Q. (1992). *Psychology*, 2nd ed. Boston: Allyn and Bacon.

Blakey, E., & Spence, S. (1990). Developing metacognition. [On-Line.] Available: Metacog.dig@www.valdosta.peachnet.edu

Brown, A., Campoine, J., & Barclay, C. (1979). Training self-checking routines for estimation test readiness: Generalization from list learning to prose recall. *Child Development, 50,* 501–512.

Christensen, D. A. (1995). *Inner victory, winning strategies for managing life's transitions.* Rexburg, ID: Capacity Books.

Covey, S. (1989). The seven habits of highly effective people. New York: Simon & Schuster.

Craig, C. M. (1998). Metacognition: Facilitating academic success. In J. L. Higbee & P. L. Dwinell, *Developmental education: Preparing successful college students* (pp. 111–112). University of South Carolina: National Association for Developmental Education.

Davidson, James West, et al. (1999) *Nation of nations: A concise narrative of the American republic,* 2nd ed. Boston: McGraw-Hill College.

El-Hindi, A. E. (1992). Enhancing metacognitive awareness of college learners. *Reading Horizons, 36,* 214–230.

Ellis, D. (1997). *Becoming a master student,* 8th ed. Boston: Houghton Mifflin.

Feldman, Robert S. (1999). *Understanding Psychology.* Boston: McGraw-Hill College.

Galzier, T. F. (1993). *The least you should know about vocabulary building.* Ft. Worth, TX: Harcourt Brace Jovanovich.

Garner, R. (1994). Metacognition and executive control. In R. B. Ruddell, M. R. Ruddell, & H. Singer (Eds.), *Theoretical models and processes of reading* (pp. 715–732). Newark, DE: International Reading Association.

Gregory, Hamilton. (1999). *Public speaking for college and career,* 5th ed. Boston: McGraw-Hill College.

Higbee, K. L. (1993). *Your memory: How it works and how to improve it,* 2nd ed. New York: Paragon House.

Jenkins, J., Matlock, B., & Slocum, T. (1989). Two approaches to vocabulary instruction: The teaching of individual word meanings and practice in deriving word meaning from context. *Reading Research Quarterly, 24,* 215–235.

Kamien, Roger. (2000). *Music: An appreciation,* 7th ed. Boston: McGraw-Hill College.

Meyers, David G. (1999). *Social psychology.* Boston: McGraw-Hill College.

Miller, G. A. (1965). The magical number seven, plus or minus two: Some limits on our capacity to process information. *Psychology Review, 63,* 81–97.

Myers, D. S. (1995). *Psychology.* Holland, MI: Worth Publishers.

Nist, S. L. & Simpson, M. L. (1988). The effectiveness and efficiency of training college students to annotate and underline text. *National Reading Conference Yearbook, 37,* 251–257.

Palinscar, A. S. & Brown, D. A. (1987). Enhancing instructional time through attention to metacognition. *Journal of Learning Disabilities, 20,* 66–75.

Paris, S. G., Wasik, B. A., & Turner, J. C. (1991). The development of student readers. In D. Pearson, R. Burr, M. Kamil, & P. Mosthenthal (Eds.), *Handbook of Reading Research* (pp. 609–640). New York: Longman.

Peterson, L. R., & Peterson, M. J. (1959). Short-term retention of individual verbal items. *Journal of Experimental Psychology, 58,* 193–198.

Peterson, S. E. (1992). The cognitive function of underlining as a study technique. *Reading Research and Instruction, 31* (2), 49–59.

Reeves, A., & Sperling, G. (1986). Attention gating in short-term retention of individual verbal items. *Psychological Review, 93,* 180–206.

Reitman, J. S. (1974). Without surreptitious rehearsal, information in short-term memory decays. *Journal of Verbal Learning and Verbal Behavior, 13,* 365–377.

Smith, B. D. (1997). *Bridging the gap,* 5th ed. New York: Longman.

Troth, D. C. (1979). A ten-minute observation in the library. *Schools and Society, 29,* 336–338.

Vacca, R. T., & Vacca, J. L. (1989). *Content area reading,* 3rd ed. New York: Harper Collins.

Weiner, B. (1986). *An attributional theory of motivation and emotion.* New York: Springer-Verlag.

Wellman, H. M. (1983). Metamemory revisited. In M. T. H. Chi (Ed.), *Trends in memory development research* (p. 32). Baselm, Switzerland: Karger.

Instructions for tearing out and folding BICUM bookmarks

Tear out one of your bookmarks along the perforated line. Fold in half along the center black line so that the four panels are on the inside. Then fold in half again lengthwise. The word BICUM should be on the front panel of your bookmark.

get *Ready*

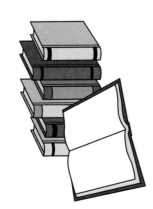

- Inventory **SELF**
  Study area
  Emotions
  Level of difficulty
  Feeling physically

- Preview

- Select or Create Questions

- Set Study Length

- Place Control ☐'s

Read

- Be Active

- Stop at ☐'s and Test Understanding

Yes, I do understand

No, I don't understand

- Determine key information

- Predict test questions

- Mark & highlight text

- Use fix-up strategies
  1. Reread
  2. Read ahead
  3. Define unfamiliar words
  4. Read out loud
  5. Mark with "?" to clear up later

Continue to next ☐

Reduce

- Post View

- Answer Questions

- Organize for Recall

(Select 1)

– make outlines

– take notes

– write summaries

– create maps

Retain

- Teach Someone

- Study in Groups

- Recreate in Writing

- Make Study Cards

- Use Mnemonics

- Rehearse

Taking Control
of Your College
Reading

•••••••●●●●●•••••

4 *R*'s for
Remembering
What You Read:

Ready
Read
Reduce
Retain

Be In Control
Use Metacognition
BICUM